CROCHET
NORO

CROCHET NORO

30 DAZZLING DESIGNS

sixth&spring books
NEW YORK

sixth&spring books

161 Avenue of the Americas
New York, New York 10013
sixthandspringbooks.com

Editorial Director	**JOY AQUILINO**
Senior Editor	**MICHELLE BREDESON**
Yarn Editor	**CHRISTINA BEHNKE**
Instructions Editors	**RANDY CAVALIERE**
	ROBYN CHACHULA
	KJ HAY
	AMY POLCYN
Instructions Proofreaders	**ROBYN CHACHULA**
	BARBARA VAN ELSEN
	CHARLES VOTH
Technical Illustrations	**ROBYN CHACHULA**
	CHARLES VOTH
Photography	**ROSE CALLAHAN**
Stylist	**KHALIAH JONES**
Hair and Makeup	**INGEBORG K.**

Vice President, Publisher	**TRISHA MALCOLM**
Creative Director	**JOE VIOR**
Production Manager	**DAVID JOINNIDES**
President	**ART JOINNIDES**

CROCHET NORO
30 Dazzling Designs
Sixth&Spring Books

ISBN 13: 978-1-936096-48-0

Library of Congress Control Number: 2012941912

Manufactured in China

1 3 5 7 9 10 8 6 4 2
First Edition

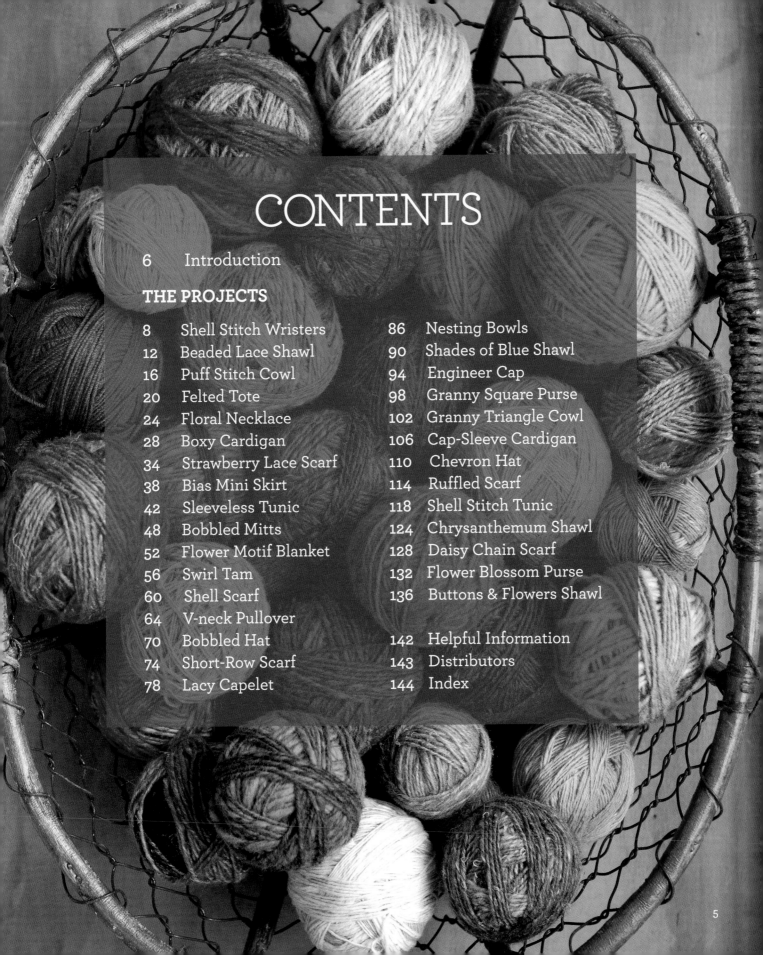

CONTENTS

INTRODUCTION

Knit Noro and its follow-up, *Knit Noro Accessories,* stretched the possibilities of Noro yarns in showcasing a breathtaking array of designs by knitting's top talents. Now, *Crochet Noro* brings together many of today's favorite crochet designers and one of the world's best-loved yarns to create a collection of incomparable beauty and originality. From exquisite shawls to stylish cardigans to quick-to-crochet accessories to fabulous bags and totes, this book contains plenty of gorgeous projects to entice every crocheter.

Eisaku Noro has been creating his world-renowned yarns in Japan's Aichi province for more than forty years. Spun from the finest natural materials with great respect for environmental concerns, these spectacular yarns are dyed exclusively by hand into a dazzling array of colors. The patterns in this artful collection employ several popular Noro yarns, including *Silk Garden, Silk Garden Lite, Silk Garden Sock, Taiyo, Taiyo Sock, Kureyon,* and *Shiraito.*

When we approached some of our favorite designers about creating original crocheted designs in Noro yarns, we were overwhelmed by their enthusiastic response. The prolific designer Yoko Hatta contributed a staggering variety of designs, including shawls, cardigans, and accessories. Robyn Chachula's elegant openwork scarf brings out the best qualities of *Shiraito.* Lily Chin, Dora Ohrenstein, and Linda Permann wowed us with their innovative hat designs. Candi Jensen's granny square purse and Marty Miller's felted tote are fun to crochet and even more fun to carry. Doris Chan and Mary Beth Temple make excellent use of their garment construction expertise to create a playful miniskirt and a flattering V-neck pullover, respectively. With patterns for every skill level, sumptuous full-color photography, clear instructions, and detailed stitch diagrams, *Crochet Noro* brings these designs to life and makes it easy to create them yourself.

If you aren't already hooked on Noro, you will be.

Shell Stitch Wristers

Shell Stitch Wristers

Gauntlet-length cuffs, a pretty shell stitch pattern punctuated with sewn-on beads, and a delicate picot edging make for hands-down the most elegant way to keep your wrists warm.

Designed by Mary Jane Hall

Skill Level: ■■■□

Materials

- 1 3½oz/100g skein (each approx 328yd/300m) of Noro *Silk Garden Sock* (wool/silk/nylon/mohair) in #272 greys/lime/brown **2**
- Size F/5 (3.75mm) crochet hook OR SIZE TO OBTAIN GAUGE
- 60 6mm Miracle Beads in #6MX872 light green
- Beading needle

Sizes

Instructions are written for size Small/Medium. Changes for sizes Large/Extra Large are in parentheses. (Shown in size Small/Medium.)

Finished Measurements

7½ (8½)" diameter at ribbing x 7½ (7½)" long/19 (21.5)cm x 19 (19)cm

Gauges

20 sts to 3½"/9cm over hdc using size F/5 (3.75mm) crochet hook.
14 rows to 4"/10cm over hdc using size F/5 (3.75mm) crochet hook.
3 5-dc shells to 4"/10cm over shell pat using size F/5 (3.75mm) crochet hook.
6 rows to 3¾"/9.5cm over shell pat using size F/5 (3.75mm) crochet hook.
TAKE TIME TO CHECK GAUGES.

Stitch Glossary

Picot Ch 2, sl st in first ch, sk 1 st, sl st in next st.
V-st Dc, ch 1, dc in same st.
Shell 5, 7, or 9 dc in same ch-1 sp, as directed.

Wrist Warmer

Cuff
Ch 22 loosely.
Row 1 Hdc in 3rd ch from hook and in each ch across, turn—20 hdc.
Row 2 Ch 2, hdc in back loop only of each hdc across—20 hdc.
Rep row 2 until piece measures 7½ (8½)"/cm. Fold in half, WS facing, and join ends of cuff using sl st. Fasten off. Turn to RS.

Hand
Join yarn to top edge of cuff, ch 1.
Rnd 1 Work 36 (42) sc evenly spaced around entire edge, join with sl st to first sc—36 (42) sc.
Rnd 2 Ch 1, sc in same sp, *sk 2 sc, 5 dc in next sc, sk 2 sc, sc in next sc; rep from * around, join with sl st to first sc. Do not turn—6 (7) shells.
Rnd 3 Ch 4 (counts as first dc + ch 1), dc in first sc (at base of ch-4) *ch 2, sc in center dc of shell, ch 2, sk next 2 dc, (dc, ch 1, dc) in next sc—V-st made. Rep from * around, sl st in 3rd ch of ch-4—6 (7) V-sts and 6 (7) sc.
Rnd 4 Ch 1, sl st between first 2 dc (in ch-1 sp), ch 3 (counts as first dc), 4 more dc between first 2 dc—5 dc shell made. *Sk next ch-2 sp, sc in next sc, sk next ch-2 sp, 5 dc in next ch-1 sp; rep from * around, sl st in 3rd ch of ch-3—6 (7) shells with 5 dc and 6 (7) sc.

Rnd 5 Ch 1, turn work to WS, sl st in last sc of previous rnd, turn again (to RS) and ch 4 (counts as first dc + ch 1), dc in same st (V-st made), cont by rep rnd 3 beg at *. End with sl st in 3rd ch of ch-4— 6 (7) V-sts and 6 (7) sc.

Rnd 6 Ch 1, sl st between first 2 dc (in ch-1 of V-st), ch 3, 6 more dc in same sp, *sk next ch-2 sp, sc in next sc, sk next ch-2 sp, 7 dc in next V-st; rep from * around, sl st in top of ch-3—6 (7) shells with 7 dc and 6 (7) sc.

Rnd 7 Ch 1, turn, sl st in sc of previous rnd (same as rnd 5), turn back to RS, ch 4, dc in same sp, *ch 2, sc in center dc of 7 dc shell, ch 2, sk next 3 dc, V-st in next sc; rep from * around, sl st to 3rd ch of ch-3—6 (7) V-sts and 6 (7) sc.

Following pat, work rnds 8–12 as follows:

Rnd 8 Rep rnd 6.

Rnd 9 Rep rnd 7.

Rnd 10 Rep rnd 6 working 9 dc for each shell.

Rnd 11 Rep rnd 7.

Rnd 12 Rep rnd 10. Do not fasten off.

Picot edging

Ch 1, turn to WS and sl st in last 2 sts of previous rnd, ch 1, turn back to RS, *ch 2, sl st in first ch from hook, sk 1 st, sl st in next st (picot made); rep from * around, sl st to first st, fasten off—30 (35) picots.

Finishing

Weave in ends. (Optional: Sew a single st between thumb and forefinger—between shells—to create thumb opening.)

Beads

Cut a strand of yarn 96"/243cm long and thread on beading needle. From WS, secure the yarn and bring up the needle to the right of any V-st. String bead on needle and center bead at base of shell in center of V-st. Bring needle back to WS at left of V-st and secure. Cont, adding a total of 30 beads in the center of each V-st on each wrist warmer. ∎

Beaded Lace Shawl

Beaded Lace Shawl

Joining the motifs as you stitch makes finishing a snap. Adding beads makes it evening-ready.

Designed by Yoko Hatta

Skill Level: ■■■□

Materials

- 2 3½oz/100g skeins (each approx 328 yd/300m) of Noro *Silk Garden Sock* (wool/silk/nylon/mohair) in #268 green/aqua/brown ▣2▣
- Size C/2 (2.75mm) crochet hook OR SIZE TO OBTAIN GAUGE
- 504 purple glass beads, 4mm diameter
- Yarn needle

Size

Instructions are written for one size.

Finished Measurements

Shawl measures approx 14"/35.5cm wide x 45"/114.5cm long

Note

Shawl is made from 42 twelve-pointed motifs. The motifs are joined using a "join-as-you-go" technique. Refer to the assembly diagram for arrangement and joining locations of motifs.

Gauge

One motif measures about 3¾"/9.5cm across (at widest point), using C/2 (2.75mm) crochet hook. TAKE TIME TO CHECK GAUGE.

Stitch Glossary

Bsc (beaded single crochet) Insert hook in indicated space, yarn over and draw up a loop, slide bead close to hook, yarn over and draw through both loops on hook.
Note Bead should stay on back side of stitch.
picot Ch 3, sl st in top of sc just made.

First Motif

Thread 12 beads onto the working yarn before beginning each motif. Ch 4; join with sl st in first ch to form a ring.
Rnd 1 (RS) Ch 1, sc in ring, [ch 3, sc in ring] 5 times; join with ch 1, hdc in first sc (counts as ch-3 sp)—6 sc, and 6 ch-3 sps.
Rnd 2 (RS) Ch 1, sc in first ch-3 sp (formed by join), picot, [ch 5, sc in next ch-3 sp, picot] 5 times; join with ch 2, dc in first sc (counts as ch-5 sp)—6 sc, and 6 ch-5 sps.
Rnd 3 (RS) Ch 1, sc in first ch-5 sp (formed by join), picot, [ch 5, sc in next ch-5 sp, picot] 5 times; join with ch 2, dc in first sc (counts as ch-5 sp).
Rnd 4 (WS—beaded) Ch 1, turn, (Bsc, ch 5, Bsc) in first ch-5 sp (formed by join), [ch 5, (Bsc, ch 5, Bsc) in next ch-5 sp] 5 times; join with ch 2, dc in first sc (counts as ch-5 sp)—12 sc, and 12 ch-5 sps.
Rnd 5 (RS) Ch 1, turn, sc in first ch-5 sp (formed by join), [ch 5, sc in next ch-5 sp] 11 times, ch 5; join with sl st in first sc.
Rnd 6 (RS) Ch 1, (3 sc, ch 3, 3 sc) in each ch-5 sp around; join with sl st in first sc—12 ch-3 sps. Fasten off.

Next 41 Motifs

Work same as first motif through rnd 5—12 sc, and 12 ch-5 sps. Before working rnd 6, refer to the assembly diagram for location of motif. Identify the joining locations between the current motif and neighboring motif(s). You may assemble the motifs in any order you wish. If you assemble motifs in rows, in the order indicated in assembly diagram, each motif will be joined to at most three neighboring motifs. A motif is joined to a neighboring motif at two consecutive ch-sps.

Rnd 6 (RS—joining rnd) Ch 1, *(3 sc, ch 3, 3 sc) in each ch-5 sp (if any) to next ch-sp that needs to be joined to a neighboring motif, hold current motif and neighboring motif with WS together and sts matching, [(3 sc, ch 1, sl st in corresponding ch-3 sp of neighboring motif, ch 1, 3 sc) in next ch-5 sp] twice; rep from * until all neighboring motifs have been joined, (3 sc, ch 3, 3 sc) in each rem ch-5 sp around; join with sl st in first sc. Fasten off.

Finishing
Weave in ends. ∎

Stitch Key

•	sl st	⌠	hdc
⬯	ch	⌡	dc
+	sc		
⊕	sc with bead		

12-Point Motif

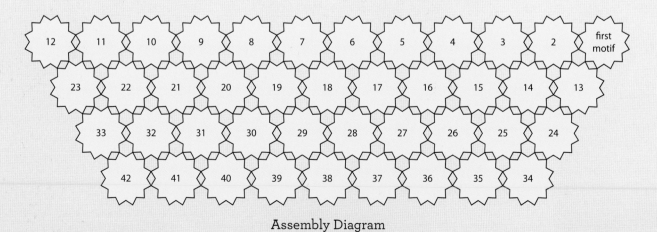

12	11	10	9	8	7	6	5	4	3	2	first motif
23	22	21	20	19	18	17	16	15	14	13
33	32	31	30	29	28	27	26	25	24
42	41	40	39	38	37	36	35	34

Assembly Diagram

Puff Stitch Cowl

Puff Stitch Cowl

Earth-toned *Kureyon* creates a gorgeous autumnal accessory. Wear it long, or double it for extra warmth.

Designed by Yoko Hatta

Skill Level: ■■□□

Materials

- 6 1¾oz/50g skeins (each approx 110yd/100m) of Noro *Kureyon* (wool) in #149 brown/grey/taupe 〔4〕
- Size G/7 (4.5mm) crochet hook OR SIZE TO OBTAIN GAUGE
- Yarn needle

Size

Instructions are written for one size.

Finished Measurements

Cowl measures approx 13"/33cm wide x 56¼"/143.5cm in circumference

Gauge

15 sts and 6⅛ rows to 4"/10cm over pattern st using G/7 (4.5mm) crochet hook. TAKE TIME TO CHECK GAUGE.

Stitch Glossary

V-st (V stitch) (Dc, ch 1, dc) in indicated stitch or space.
Puff-st (Puff stitch) [Yarn over, insert hook in indicated space and draw up a loop] 3 times, yarn over and draw through all 7 loops on hook, ch 1 (to close puff, does not count as a separate stitch).
Puff-V (Puff V stitch) (Puff, ch 1, Puff) in indicated space.

Cowl

Ch 52.

Row 1 (RS) Dc in 4th ch from hook (beg ch counts as dc), *sk next 2 ch, V-st in next ch; rep from * across to last 3 ch, sk next 2 ch, 2 dc in last ch—15 V-sts, and 2 dc at each end.

Row 2 Ch 3 (counts as dc here and throughout), turn, sk next dc, V-st in sp between first 2 dc and first V-st, *V-st in next sp between V-sts; rep from * across to last V-st, V-st in sp between last V-st and last 2 dc, dc in top of turning ch—16 V-sts, and 1 dc at each end.

Row 3 Ch 3, turn, Puff-V in ch-1 sp of each V-st across, dc in top of turning ch—16 Puff-V sts, and 1 dc at each end.

Row 4 Ch 3, turn, V-st in ch-1 sp of each Puff-V across, dc in top of turning ch—16 V-sts, and 1 dc at each end.

Row 5 Ch 3, turn, dc in first dc, sk sp between first dc and first V-st, V-st in each sp between V-sts across, sk sp between last V-st and last dc, 2 dc in top of turning ch—15 V-sts and 2 dc at each end.

Rows 6–89 Rep last 4 rows 21 times.

Rows 90–92 Rep rows 2–4.

Fasten off.

Edging

With RS facing, join yarn with sl st in corner to work across a long side edge, *ch 3, sl st in end of next row (working into the top of the dc or ch-3 at the end of the row); rep from * across side edge to corner. Fasten off. Rep edging across other long side edge.

Finishing

Sew short ends together. Weave in ends. ■

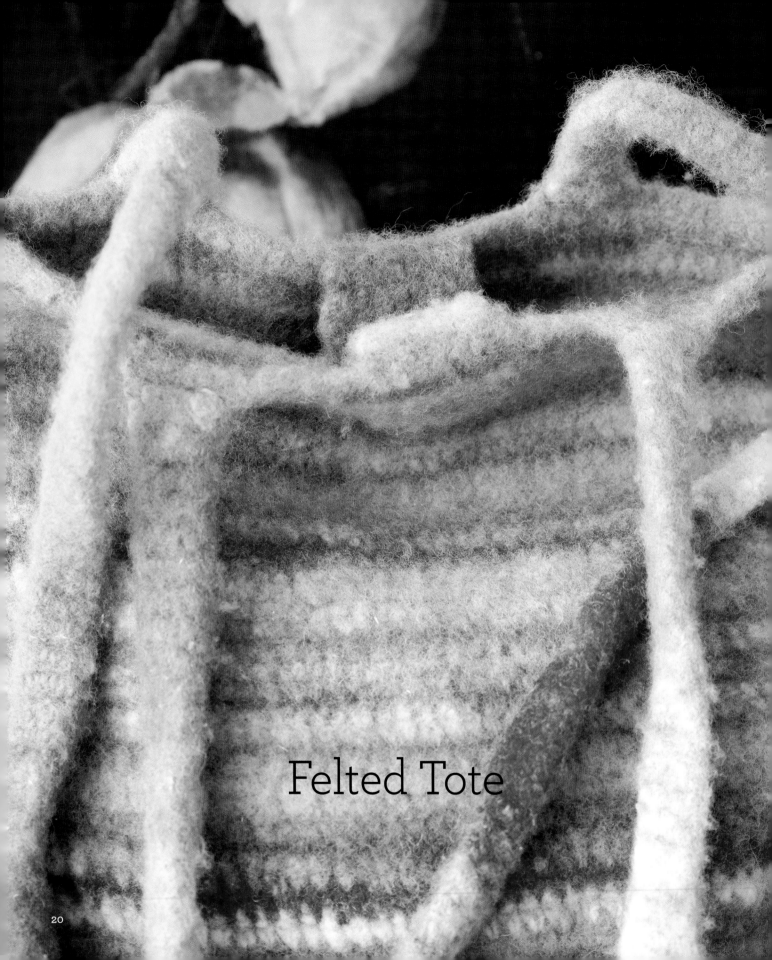

Felted Tote

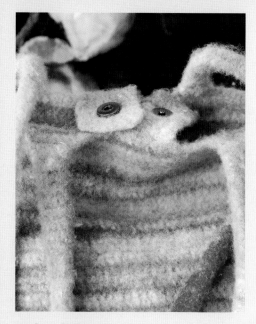

Felted Tote

Vibrant shades of *Kureyon* soften and blend after felting into a harmonious palette, making this sturdy tote as pretty as it is practical.

Designed by Marty Miller

Skill Level: ■■□□

Materials

- 6 1¾oz/50g skeins (each approx 110yd/100m) of Noro *Kureyon* (wool) in #287 plum/greens/marigold/brown (**4**)
- Size L/11 (8mm) crochet hook
  OR SIZE TO OBTAIN GAUGE
- Locking stitch markers
- Yarn needle
- Zippered pillowcase (for felting)
- ¾"/19mm magnetic snap closure (Clover Art No. 6245; optional)

Size

Instructions are written for one size.

Finished Measurements

17"/43cm wide x 15½"/39.5cm tall (before felting)
12"/30.5cm wide x 12"/30.5cm tall (after felting)

Gauge

11 sts and 13 rows to 4"/10cm over sc using L/11 (8mm) crochet hook, before felting. TAKE TIME TO CHECK GAUGE.

Notes

1) It is very important to work loosely so that the bag will felt properly.
2) Do not join ends of rnds but work in a continuous spiral, unless otherwise directed.

Tote

Ch 46 loosely.
Rnd 1 2 sc in 2nd ch from hook, sc in each of next 43 ch, 3 sc in last ch. Working into the other side of the foundation ch, skip the ch with 3 sc just worked, sc in each of the next 43 ch, sc in the last sc, pm—92 sc.
Rnd 2 Sc in each sc around.
Rnds 3–50 Rep rnd 2. Fasten off. At the end of rnd 50, before fastening off, fold the tote flat and pm at the opposite side edge. Leave markers in place.

Handles (make 2)

Ch 9.
Row 1 Sc in the 2nd ch from the hook and in each ch across—8 sc. Do *not* turn.
Rnd 2 Beg working in rnds in sc.
Rnd 3 Sc in each sc around.
Rep rnd 3 until piece measures 35"/89cm. Fasten off, leaving a long tail for sewing.

Finishing

Mark 8 sts in from each marker on front and back of tote. Flatten ends of handles and join to tote at markers with sc, one handle on each side. Weave in ends.

Flaps (optional)

Mark center 8 sts on each side of tote. WS facing, join yarn and work as follows on each side, on marked sts only:
Row 1 Working in front loops only, sc in the first sc, and in each of the next 7 sc, to last marker. Ch 1, turn.
Row 2 Working through both loops, sc in the first sc, and in each of the next 7 sc. Ch 1, turn.
Rows 3–8 Rep row 2. Fasten off. Weave in ends.

Felting

Place tote in pillowcase. Place in washing machine with lowest water level and hot water. Add a small amount of detergent and old towels or jeans to help agitate. Start cycle, checking bag every 5 minutes until desired size is achieved. Shape and dry flat.
Following package instructions, attach snap to flaps. ■

Floral Necklace

Floral Necklace

Four flowered strands embellished with beads create a fresh-as-spring accessory to liven up your look.

Designed by Linda Permann

Skill Level: ■■■☐

Materials

- 1 3½oz/100g skein (each approx 462yd/422m) of Noro *Taiyo Sock* (cotton/wool/nylon/silk) in #8 teals/grey/khaki ❶
- Size E/4 (3.5mm) crochet hook OR SIZE TO OBTAIN GAUGE
- 63 6mm round beads in Bead Chalk Turquoise (#H20-7639GS at firemountaingems.com)
- Beading needle
- ½"/12mm button

Size

Instructions are written for one size.

Finished Measurements

26½"/67cm long at shortest strand; 34"/86.5cm long at longest strand.

Gauge

Large flowers measure 1½"/4cm in diameter.

Stitch Glossary

B-ch (beaded chain) Slide bead up to working loop, yo, allowing bead to fall to back of work, draw through loop on hook.
tr2tog (treble crochet 2 together) (Yo twice and insert hook in st, yo and draw up a loop, [yo and draw through first two loops on hook] twice) twice, yo and draw through rem 3 loops on hook.
dc2tog (double crochet 2 together) (Yo and insert hook in st, yo and draw up a loop, yo and draw through first two loops on hook) twice, yo and draw through rem 3 loops on hook.

Notes

1) Necklace is constructed in a continuous manner to create 4 connected strands. Since necklace requires very little yarn, feel free to wind off undesirable colors and change colors at the end of rows for more contrast. If using this technique, divide beads and thread before starting each strand, threading 11 (19, 15, 23) beads onto yarn before beginning each strand. Be careful not to twist crocheted strands when connecting strands with single crochet.
2) Use care when sliding beads along yarn, gently sliding just a few beads at a time to prevent yarn from breaking.

Necklace

String 63 beads onto yarn.
Strand 1 Ch 20, place marker in 10th ch from hook, *B-ch, ch 12, work (tr2tog, ch 3, sl st, [ch 3, tr2tog, ch 3, sl st] 4 times) in 4th ch from hook, reinsert hook in center hole of flower, B-ch, bring hook back through to front of flower, placing hook between 2 petals directly across from original ch, ch 7; rep from * 4 times, B-ch, ch 20, join with sl st in first ch—5 flowers, 6 B-ch.
Strand 2 Ch 1, turn, sc in back bump only of first 10 ch, ch 5, *B-ch, ch 8, work (dc2tog, ch 2, sl st, [ch 2, dc2tog, ch 2, sl st] 2 times) in third ch from hook, reinsert hook in center hole of flower, B-ch, bring hook back through to front of flower, placing hook between 2 petals directly across from original ch, ch 5; rep from * 8 times, B-ch,

ch 5, sc in back bump only of marked st from strand 1 and next 9 ch—9 flowers, 10 B-ch, 20 sc.

Strand 3 Ch 1, turn, sc in each of previous 10 sc, ch 10, *B-ch, ch 12, work (tr2tog, ch 3, sl st, [ch 3, tr2tog, ch 3, sl st] 4 times) in 4th ch from hook, reinsert hook in center hole of flower, B-ch, bring hook back through to front of flower, placing hook between 2 petals directly across from original ch, ch 7; rep from * 6 times, B-ch, ch 10, sc in each of next 10 sc—7 flowers, 8 B-ch, 20 sc.

Strand 4 Ch 1, turn, sc in 10 sc, ch 5, *B-ch, ch 8, work (dc2tog, ch 2, sl st, [ch 2, dc2tog, ch 2, sl st] 2 times) in 3rd ch from hook, reinsert hook in center hole of flower, B-ch, bring hook back through to front of flower, placing hook between 2 petals directly across from original ch, ch 5; rep from * 10 times, B-ch, ch 5, sc in each of next 10 sc, ch 5, sl st in first ch (button loop formed)—11 flowers, 12 B-ch, 20 sc, one ch-5 button loop.

Final row Ch 1, turn, sl st in each of 5 ch just made, sl st in last sc of strand 4—6 sl sts.

Fasten off, leaving a long tail for sewing.

Finishing

Whipstitch long edges of sc section together to form a tube. Rep for other end of necklace. Sew a button to end of necklace opposite of the button loop. Weave in ends. For best results, wet-block and pin each flower to shape. ∎

Boxy Cardigan

Boxy Cardigan

With its subtle black, green, and blue palette, easy shape, and single-button closure, this classic cardigan will be on every crocheter's to-stitch list.

Designed by Yoko Hatta

Skill Level: ■■■□

Materials

- 4 (5,6) 3½oz/100g skeins (each approx 328yd/300m) of Noro *Silk Garden Sock* (wool/silk/nylon/mohair) in #252 black/lime/blue ①
- Size E/4 (3.5mm) crochet hook OR SIZE TO OBTAIN GAUGE
- Stitch markers
- ¹³/₁₆"/2cm-diameter button

Sizes

Instructions are written for size Small/Medium (Large, X-Large); shown in size Small/Medium.

Finished Measurements

Bust 37½ (45¼, 47¼)"/95 (115, 120)cm
Length (from back neck) 21 (24¼, 24½)"/53.5 (62, 62)cm

Note

Cardigan is worked from the bottom up to the armholes. Sleeves are then crocheted in the round from the cuff to the armhole seam. Yoke is worked last, connecting the sleeves seamlessly to the body.

Gauge

22 dc and 9½ rows = 4½"/11.5cm in pattern stitch using size E/4 (3.5mm) crochet hook. TAKE TIME TO CHECK GAUGE.

Stitch Glossary

V-st (Dc, ch 1, dc) in indicated st

Cardigan

Body

Ch 184 (208, 232).

Row 1 (RS) Dc in 4th ch from hook and each ch across—182 (206, 230) dc.

Row 2 Ch 3 (counts as dc, here and throughout), turn, *skip 1 dc, v-st in next st, skip 1 dc; rep from * across; dc in top of beg ch—60 (68, 76) v-sts.

Row 3 Ch 3, turn, *dc in next dc, dc in ch-1 sp, dc in next dc; rep from * across, dc in top of beg ch.

Rows 4–5 Ch 3, turn, dc in ea dc across, dc in top of beg ch.

Rep rows 2–5 until body measures 12¼ (14, 14)"/20.5 (21.5, 23)cm. End with a row 5.

Sleeves

Make 2, ch 58 (64, 70), sl st to first ch to join.

Rnd 1 (WS) Ch 3, turn, *skip 1 ch, v-st in next ch, sk 1 ch; rep from * around; sl st to top of beg ch—19 (21, 23) v-sts.

Rnd 2 Ch 3, turn, *dc in next dc, dc in ch-1 sp, dc in next dc; rep from * around, sl st in top of beg ch.

Rnds 3–4 Ch 3, turn, dc in each dc around, sl st in top of beg ch.

Rnd 5 Ch 3, turn, *skip 1 dc, v-st in next dc, skip 1 dc; rep from * around, sl st in top of beg ch.

Rnds 6–9 Reps rnds 2–5.

Rnds 10–12 Rep rnds 2–4.

Rnd 13 Ch 3, turn, dc in top of beg ch, *skip 1 dc, v-st in next dc, skip 1 dc; rep from * around, dc in same st as beg ch, sl st to top of beg ch.

Rnd 14 Ch 3, dc in next dc, *dc in next dc, dc in ch-1 sp, dc in next dc; rep from * around, dc in last dc, sl st in top of beg ch—60 (66, 72) dc.

Rnds 15–16 Rep rnds 3–4.

Rnd 17 Ch 4 (counts as dc, ch-1 sp), turn, dc in top of same beg ch, *skip 2 dc, v-st in next dc; rep from * around, skip last 2 dc, ch 1, dc in same sp as beg, sl st to third ch of beg ch.

Rnd 18 Ch 3, turn, *dc in ch-1 sp, dc in next 2 dc; rep from * around, dc in last ch-1 sp, sl st to top of beg ch—62 (68, 74) dc.

Rnds 19–20 Rep rnds 3–4.

Rnd 21 Ch 3, turn, *v-st in next dc, skip 2 dc; rep from * around, v-st in last dc, sl st in top of beg ch.

Rnds 22–24 Rep rnds 2–4—64 (70, 76) dc.

Rnd 25–28 Rep rnds 13–16—66 (72, 78) dc. Fasten off.

Join sleeves

Align sleeve beg ch with 46th (52nd, 58th) st from end. Pin RS of body and sleeve together. Join yarn with sl st 4 (7, 10) sts from beg ch. Sc through both body and sleeve sts at the same time for 8 (14, 20) sts, fasten off. Repeat on opposite side.

Yoke joining

Row 1 (WS) Ch 3, turn, [skip 1 dc, v-st in next st, skip 1 dc] 12 (13, 14) times, *skip 1 dc, dc in next 2 dc, place marker in prev dc, dc in next 5 dc, place marker in prev dc, dc in next dc*, rep directions for 16 v-sts across sleeve, rep from * to *; rep direction for 24 (26, 28) v-sts across back panel, rep from * to *, rep directions for 16 v-st across sleeve, rep from * to *, rep directions for 12 (13, 14) v-sts across front panel; dc in top of beg ch—80 (84, 88) v-sts.

Yoke shaping [L/XL]

Row 2 (RS) Ch 3, turn, *dc in next dc, dc in ch-1 sp, dc in next dc; rep from * across to 1 st before marker, dc2tog over next 2 sts, move marker, **[dc in each st to marker, move marker] twice, dc in each st to marker, dc2tog over next 2 sts, move marker**, dc in each st to 1 st before marker, dc2tog over next 2 sts, move marker; rep from ** to ** once, dc in each st to beg ch, dc in top of beg ch—282 (294 dc).

Rows 3–4 Ch 3, turn, *dc in each dc to 1 st before marker, dc2tog over next 2 sts, move marker, [dc in each dc to marker, move marker] twice, dc in each st to marker, dc2tog over next 2 sts, move marker; rep from * once, dc in each st to beg ch, dc in top of beg ch—274 (286 dc).

Row 5 Ch 3, turn, *skip 1 dc, v-st in next st, skip 1 dc, rep from * across to 1 st before marker, dc in next dc, move marker, dc in each dc to marker, dc in next dc, move marker, dc in next dc; rep from * across end with dc in top of beg ch—80 (84 v-sts).

Yoke

Row 1 (RS) Ch 3, turn, *dc in next dc, dc in ch-1 sp, dc in next dc; rep from * across to 1 st before marker, dc2tog over next 2 sts, move marker, dc in each st to marker, dc2tog over next 2 sts, move marker; rep from * across, dc in each st to beg ch, dc in top of beg ch—266 (266, 278 dc).

Rows 2–3 Ch 3, turn, *dc in each dc to 1 st before marker, dc2tog over next 2 sts, move marker, dc in each dc to marker, dc2tog over next 2 sts, move marker, rep from * across, dc in each dc to beg ch, dc in top of beg ch—250 (250, 262 dc).

Row 4 Ch 3, turn, *skip 1 dc, v-st in next st, skip 1 dc, rep from * across to 3 sts before marker, dc in next dc, ch 1, dc2tog in prev dc and marked dc, move marker, dc in each dc to marker, dc2tog in marked dc and dc 3 sts away, ch 1, dc in prev dc; rep from * across end with dc in top of beg ch—72 (72, 76 v-sts).

Rows 5–7 Rep rows 1–3.

Row 8 Ch 3, turn, *skip 1 dc, v-st in next st, skip 1 dc, rep from * across to 2 sts before marker, skip next dc, dc in next 2 dc, move marker, dc in each dc to marker, dc in marked dc, move marker, dc in next dc, skip next dc; rep from * across end with dc in top of beg ch—56 (56, 60 v-sts).

Rows 9–12 Rep Rows 1–4—48 (48, 52) v-sts.

Row 13 Turn, sl st in next 6 (6, 9) sts, sc in next 2 sts, hdc in next 2 sts, *dc in next dc, dc in ch-1 sp, dc in next dc; rep from * across to 1 st before marker, dc2tog over next 2 sts, move marker, dc in each st to marker, dc2tog over next 2 sts, move marker; rep from * across to front panel, dc in each st to last 10 (10, 13) sts, hdc in next 2 sts, sc in next 2 sts, sl st in next st—134 (134, 140 dc).

Row 14 Turn, skip sl st, sl st in next 5 sts, sc in next dc, hdc in next dc, *dc in each dc to 1 st before marker, dc2tog over next 2 sts, move marker, dc in each dc to marker, dc2tog over next 2 sts, move marker, rep from * across to front panel, dc in each dc last 3 dc, hdc in next dc, sc in next dc, sl st in last dc—120 (120, 126 dc).

Row 15 Turn, skip sl st, sl st in next 3 sts, sc in next dc, ch 1, *dc in each dc to 1 st before marker, dc2tog over next 2 sts, move marker, dc in each dc to marker, dc2tog over next 2 sts, move marker, rep from * across to front panel, dc in each dc last 2 dc, ch 1, sc in next dc, sl st in last dc—108 (108, 114 dc).

Row 16 Turn, skip sl st, sl st in sc, sl st in ch-1 sp, sl st in dc, ch 2, skip next dc, v-st in next dc, skip next 2 dc, dc in each dc to marker, dc in marked dc, move marker, dc in next dc, skip next dc, *skip 1 dc, v-st in next st, skip 1 dc, rep from * across to 2 sts before marker, skip next dc, dc in next 2 dc, move marker, dc in each dc to marker, dc in marked dc, move marker, dc in next dc, skip next dc; rep from * across to last marker, skip next dc, dc in next dc, ch 1, dc2tog in prev and last dc—22 (22, 24 v-sts).

Row 17 Ch 3, turn, dc in ch-1 sp, dc in next dc, dc2tog over next 2 sts, dc in each dc to marker, dc2tog over next 2 sts, move marker, *dc in next dc, dc in ch-1 sp, dc in next dc; rep from * across to 1 st before marker, dc2tog over next 2 sts, move marker, dc in each st to marker, dc2tog over next 2 sts, move marker; rep from * across to last 3 sts, dc in next dc, dc2tog over last 2 sts—94 (94, 100 dc).

Row 18 Ch 2, turn, skip first 2 sts, hdc in next st, dc in each dc to marker, dc2tog over next 2 sts, move marker, *dc in each dc to 1 st before marker, dc2tog over next 2 sts, move marker, dc in each dc to marker, dc2tog over next 2 sts, move marker, rep from * across to last 3 sts, hdc2tog over next and last st, fasten off—76 (76, 82 dc).

Row 19 Turn, skip 10 sts, join yarn with sl st to next dc, sc in next dc, hdc in next 2 dc, dc in next dc, dc2tog over next 2 dc, dc in each dc to marker, dc2tog over next 2 sts, move marker, dc in each dc to 1 st before marker, dc2tog over next 2 sts, move marker, dc in next dc, hdc in next 2 dc, sc in next dc, sl st to next dc—46 (46, 52 dc).

Row 20 Turn, skip sl st, sl st in next 4 sts, sc in next st, hdc in next st, dc in each dc to marker, dc2tog in marked dc and dc 3 sts away, ch 1, dc in prev dc, *skip 1 dc, v-st in next st, skip 1 dc, rep from * across to 3 sts before marker, dc in next dc, ch 1, dc2tog in prev dc and marked dc, move marker, dc in next 3 dc, hdc in next dc, sc in next dc, sl st in next dc, fasten off—10 (10, 12) v-sts.

Sleeve cuff edging

With RS facing, join yarn to edge of cuff with sl st, ch 1, sc evenly around cuff in a multiple of 3 sts, sl st to first sc. Turn, *ch 3, skip 2 sc, sl st in next sc; rep from * around, fasten off.

Neck and body edging

With RS facing, join yarn to edge of front panel at bottom edge with sl st, ch 1, sc evenly across in a multiple of 3 sts to last 2 rows before top of right front panel, ch 4, skip last 2 rows, sc evenly around neck, opposite front panel, bottom edge, sl st to first sc. Turn, *ch 3, skip 2 sc, sl st in next sc; rep from * around to buttonhole, ch 3, sl st in ch-4 sp, ch 3, sl st in next sc, rep from * around, fasten off.

Block lightly, if desired. Weave in ends. ∎

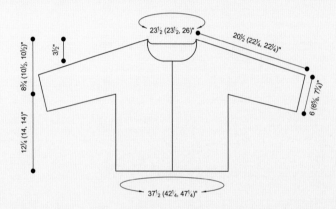

Strawberry Lace Scarf

Strawberry Lace Scarf

Fine-weight yarn in a blend of cashmere, angora, and wool creates a deliciously light and lacy scarf with a sweet motif.

Designed by Robyn Chachula

Skill Level: ■■□□

Materials

- 2 hanks 1¾/oz/50g skeins (each approx 198yd/181m) of Noro *Shiraito* (cashmere/angora/wool) in #8 pinks/greens/purple/red ❶
- Size G/6 (4mm) crochet hook OR SIZE TO OBTAIN GAUGE
- Yarn needle

Size

Instructions are written for one size.

Finished Measurements

Approx 7"/18cm wide x 72"/183cm long (excluding fringe)

Note

There are 2 stitch repeats worked across the width of the scarf. Each repeat consists of a "strawberry" and the stitches on each side of the strawberry.

Gauge

One stitch repeat and 8 rows to 3½"/9cm over "strawberry" pattern stitch using G/6 (4mm) crochet hook. TAKE TIME TO CHECK GAUGE.

Stitch Glossary

shell ([Dc, ch 1] 4 times, dc) in indicated stitch.
V-st (V stitch) (Dc, ch 1, dc) in indicated stitch.

Scarf

Ch 40.

Row 1 (RS) Sc in 12th ch from hook (beg ch counts as 3 foundation ch, dc, ch 5), [ch 3, sk next ch, sc in next ch] 4 times, ch 5, sk next 3 ch, dc in next ch, ch 5, sk next 3 ch, sc in next ch, [ch 3, sk next ch, sc in next ch] 4 times, ch 5, sk next 3 ch, dc in last ch—2 groups of 4 ch-3 sps each (2 pattern repeats).

Row 2 Ch 8 (counts as dc, ch 5), turn, sk first ch-5 sp, sc in next ch-3 sp, [ch 3, sc in next ch-3 sp] 3 times, ch 5, sk next ch-5 sp, dc in next dc, ch 5, sk next ch-5 sp, sc in next ch-3 sp, [ch 3, sc in next ch-3 sp] 3 times, ch 5, dc in 6th ch of beg ch.

Row 3 Ch 3 (counts as dc), turn, dc in first dc, ch 5, sk first ch-5 sp, sc in next ch-3 sp, [ch 3, sc in next ch-3 sp] twice, ch 5, sk next ch-5 sp, V-st in next dc, ch 5, sk next ch-5 sp, sc in next ch-3 sp, [ch 3, sc in next ch-3 sp] twice, ch 5, 2 dc in 3rd ch of turning ch.

Row 4 Ch 4 (counts as dc, ch 1), turn, V-st in first dc, ch 5, sk first ch-5 sp, sc in next ch-3 sp, ch 3, sc in next ch-3 sp, ch 5, sk next ch-5 sp, shell in ch-1 sp of next V-st, ch 5, sk next ch-5 sp, sc in next ch-3 sp, ch 3, sc in next ch-3 sp, ch 5, sk next ch-5 sp, ([dc, ch 1] twice, dc) in top of turning ch.

Row 5 Ch 1, turn, sc in first dc, [ch 3, sk next ch-1 sp, sc in next dc] twice, ch 5, sk next ch-5 sp, dc in next ch-3 sp, ch 5, sk next ch-5 sp, sc in next dc, [ch 3, sk next ch-1 sp, sc in next dc] 4 times, ch 5, sk next ch-5 sp, dc in next ch-3 sp, ch 5, sk next ch-5 sp, sc in next dc, ch 3, sk next ch-1 sp, sc in next dc, ch 3, sc in 3rd ch of turning ch, turn.

Row 6 Ch 4, turn, sc in first ch-3 sp, ch 3, sc in next ch-3 sp, ch 5, sk next ch-5 sp, dc in next dc, ch 5, sk next ch-5 sp, sc in next ch-3 sp, [ch 3, sc in next ch-3 sp] 3 times, ch 5, sk next ch-5 sp, dc in next dc, ch 5, sk next ch-5 sp, sc in next ch-3 sp, ch 3, sc in next ch-3 sp, ch 1, dc in last sc.

Row 7 Ch 1, turn, sc in first dc, ch 3, sc in next ch-3 sp, ch 5, sk next ch-5 sp, V-st in next dc, ch 5, sk next ch-5 sp, sc in next ch-3 sp, [ch 3, sc in next ch-3 sp] twice, ch 5, sk next ch-5 sp, V-st in next dc, ch 5, sk next ch-5 sp, sc in next ch-3 sp, ch 3, sc in 3rd ch of beg ch.

Row 8 Ch 4, turn, sc in first ch-3 sp, ch 5, sk next ch-5 sp, shell in ch-1 sp of next V-st, ch 5, sk next ch-5 sp, sc in next ch-3 sp, ch 3, sc in next ch-3 sp, ch 5, sk next ch-5 sp, shell in ch-1 sp of next V-st, ch 5, sk next ch-5 sp, sc in next ch-3 sp, ch 1, dc in last sc.

Row 9 Ch 8 (counts as dc, ch 5), turn, sk first ch-5 sp, sc in next dc, [ch 3, sk next ch-1 sp, sc in next dc] 4 times, ch 5, sk next ch-5 sp, dc in next ch-3 sp, ch 5, sk next ch-5 sp, sc in next dc, [ch 3, sc in next dc] 4 times, ch 5, sk next ch-5 sp, dc in 3rd ch of beg ch.

Rows 10–161 Rep rows 2–9, 19 times.

Rows 162–164 Rep rows 2–4.

Row 165 Ch 1, turn, sc in first dc, ch 1, sk next ch-1 sp, hdc in next dc, ch 1, sk next ch-1 sp, dc in next dc, ch 5, sk next ch-5 sp, tr in next ch-3 sp, ch 5, sk next ch-5 sp, dc in next dc, ch 1, sk next ch-1 sp, hdc in next dc, ch 1, sk next ch-1 sp, sc in next dc, ch 1, sk next ch-1 sp, hdc in next dc, ch 1, sk next ch-1 sp, dc in next dc, ch 5, sk next ch-5

sp, tr in next ch-3 sp, ch 5, sk next ch-5 sp, dc in next dc, ch 1, sk next ch-1 sp, hdc in next dc, ch 1, sc in 3rd ch of turning ch.

Edging (RS) Ch 1, do not turn, beg across long side edge, work sc evenly spaced all the way around the outer edge of the scarf, working 3 sc in each corner; join with sl st in first sc. Fasten off.

Finishing

Weave in ends. Pin scarf to schematic measurements and spray with water. Allow piece to dry.

Fringe

Attach 9 fringes evenly spaced across each short edge of scarf, as follows: Cut 90 strands of yarn, each 22"/56cm long. Hold 5 strands together, and fold in half. Insert hook in edge of scarf, place fold on hook and draw through, forming a loop. Thread ends of strands through loop and pull to tighten. Rep to attach 9 fringes across each short edge. Divide each fringe into 2 groups of 5 strands each. Beg with 2nd set of 5-strands, hold neighboring groups of 5 strands together and tie an overhand knot about 1"/2.5cm below edge. Rep to knot all fringes (except first and last 5-strand sets). Divide the new groups into 2 groups of 5 strands each. Beg with first set of 5-strands, hold neighboring groups of 5 strands together and tie an overhand knot about 1"/2.5cm below last row of knots. Rep to knot all fringes. Trim fringes. ∎

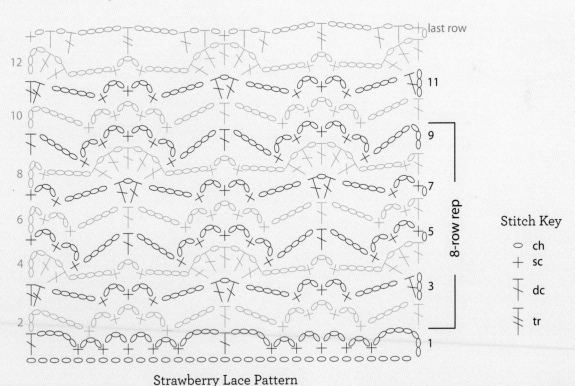

Strawberry Lace Pattern

Stitch Key

∘ ch
+ sc
┬ dc
┬ tr

8-row rep

Bias Miniskirt

Bias Miniskirt

The body of this fetching skirt is a not-quite-parallelogram, worked on the bias. It is seamlessly assembled into a tube while working the last row.

Designed by Doris Chan

Skill Level: ■■■□

Materials

- 4 (5, 6) 1¾oz/50g balls (each approx 137yd/125m) of Noro *Silk Garden Lite* (silk/mohair/lambswool) in #2012 olive/purples/salmon (3)
- Size H/8 (5mm) crochet hook for body OR SIZE TO OBTAIN GAUGE
- Size G/7 (4.5mm) crochet hook for waistband OR SIZE TO OBTAIN GAUGE
- Stitch markers
- 1 50yd/45cm card of 1mm (fine) elastic (Rainbow Elastic/Bryson Distributing, #50 olive)
- Yarn needle

Sizes

Instructions are written for sizes Small (Medium, Large); shown in size Small.

Finished Measurements

Waist circumference 26 (30, 34)"/66 (76, 86.5)cm
Hip circumference 36 (40, 44)"/91.5 (101.5, 112)cm
Length 17 (18½, 20)"/43 (47, 51)cm

Notes

1) An additional skein or two of *Silk Garden Lite* is recommended for adjusting color distribution.
2) Working with elastic: Choose the shade of elastic that most closely matches the yarn color that will appear at the top of the waistband. Hold one strand of elastic together with one strand of yarn. Try to keep both strands feeding smoothly at the same tension to avoid overly stretching the elastic. The strands will naturally twist around each other; simply work through the twisting. Weave in the ends of elastic in the same way as yarn ends.

Gauges

12 Fsc with ch-3 sps = 4"/10cm using size H/8 (5mm) hook.
In stitch pattern, 4 repeats (3dc-cl, ch 1) or 4 Vst = 3"/7.5cm and 8 rows = 4"/10cm (measured perpendicularly at the center of rows, away from the ends) using size H/8 (5mm) crochet hook.
13 hdc = 4"/10cm, and 9 rounds = 3"/7.5cm crochet over hdcflo of band using size G/6 (4mm) crochet hook. TAKE TIME TO CHECK GAUGES.

Stitch Glossary

Basic Fsc (foundation single crochet) Note Basic stitch for reference only; skirt foundation will be slightly different. Ch 2, insert hook in 2nd ch from hook, yo and draw up a loop, yo and draw through one loop (foundation chain made, place marker), yo and draw through 2 loops (Fsc made). Working into marked chain and leaving 2 strands along the chain edge of the foundation, *insert hook through 2 strands of the foundation chain (under the nub at the back of that chain), yo and draw up a loop, yo and draw through one loop (foundation chain made, move marker), yo and draw through 2 loops (Fsc made). Repeat from * for desired number of Fsc.
3dc-cl (double crochet bobble) [Yo, insert hook into indicated st/sp, yo and draw up a loop, yo and draw through 2 loops on hook] 3 times in same st or sp indicated, yo and draw through all 4 loops on hook.

V-st (Hdc, ch 1, hdc) in st or sp indicated.

Hdctbl (half-double crochet through the back loop only) Yo, insert hook in back loop of next hdc, yo and draw up a loop, yo and draw through all 3 loops on hook.

Hdctbl-dec (half-double crochet through the back loop only decrease) Yo, insert hook through the back loop of next hdc, yo and draw up a loop, insert hook through the back loop of next hdc, yo and draw up a loop, yo and draw through all 4 loops on hook.

The following two rows of stitch pattern, a RS row of bobbles and a WS row of V-sts, create increases every row at the waist edge and decreases every row at the hem edge.

Bobble Row (RS; begins at waist edge) Ch 5, turn, skip first dc, 3dc-cl in next ch-1 sp, [ch 1, 3dc-cl in ch-1 sp of next V-st] across to last V-st, end with ch 5, sc in ch-1 sp of last V-st.

V-st Row (WS; begins at hem edge) Ch 4, turn, sc in next ch-5 sp of edge, ch 4, [skip next 3dc-cl, V-st in next ch-1 sp] across to last 3dc-cl, skip last 3dc-cl, end with (V-st, ch 1, dc) in ch-5 tch sp.

Skirt

Bias body

Note The skirt body begins with a row of Fsc interspersed with ch-3 spaces worked as you go. This creates a sturdy foundation that equals a V-st row and has as much elasticity as the stitch pattern used for the body.

Row 1 (Foundation row) (WS) Ch 4, insert hook in 4th ch from hook, yo and draw up a loop, yo and draw through one loop on hook, yo and draw through 2 loops on hook (first Fsc made), Fsc; [ch 3, skip 3 ch just made, Fsc twice] 21 (23, 25) times, ch 3, skip 3 ch just made, Fsc once, ch 1, dc in ch of last Fsc made—45 Fsc with one ch-4 edge sp, 22 (24, 26) ch-3 sps, one ending ch-1 sp.

Note Foundation row should measure approximately 16"/40cm. Place marker in the base of the 2nd to last Fsc made and leave for assembly later.

Row 2 Ch 5, turn, skip first dc, 3dc-cl in next ch-1 sp, [ch 1, 3dc-cl in next ch-3 sp] 22 (24, 26) times, end with ch 5, sc in ch-4 edge sp—23 (25, 27) bobbles.

Row 3 Work V-st row—23 (25, 27) V-sts plus one ending ch-1 sp.

Rows 4–51 (59, 67) Alternate Bobble row and V-st row 24 (28, 32) times.

Body assembly

Turn, with RS facing, bring the last row of V-sts made tog with the foundation edge, fold the body into a tube, connect the edges while working the assembly row of bobbles, bouncing back and forth from working row to foundation edge.

Assembly row (RS) Beg at waist edge, ch 3, insert hook from front to back in marked Fsc of row 1, sl st in marked Fsc, ch 1, skip first dc of working row, 3dc-cl in next ch-1 sp, sk next Fsc on row 1, [sl st in next Fsc, ch 1, 3dc-cl in ch-1 sp of next V-st, skip next Fsc on row 1] 21 (23, 25) times, end with sl st in last Fsc on row 1, ch 1, 3dc-cl in ch-1 sp of next V-st, ch 5, sc in ch-1 sp of last V-st of working row, turn, ch 4, sc in ch-5 sp just made, ch 4, sl st in ch-4 edge sp of row 1 at hem edge, fasten off—23 (25, 27) bobbles.

Waistband

Return to waist edge of body tube. Switch to smaller hook and work to a slightly firmer gauge. Waistband is worked with RS always facing in spiral fashion, not joined or turned. This minimizes the jog in the color striping from round to round. In rnd 1 make 2 stitches in each of 52 (60, 68) row edges of body tube, gently gathering the waist edge.

Rnd 1 (RS) Join yarn in any row edge of body tube at waist, ch 1, sc in same row edge, 2 hdc in each row edge around, end with hdc in same row edge as beginning sc—104 (120, 136) stitches. Place marker in beginning st of each round, move marker up as you go. Begin shaping the band with 4 decreases evenly spaced around.

Rnd 2 Hdctbl in first sc, move marker up, hdctbl in each of next 23 (27, 31) hdc, (hdctbl-dec in next 2 hdc, hdctbl in each of next 24 (28, 32) hdc) 3 times, hdctbl-dec in last 2 hdc—100 (116, 132) hdc.

Rnd 3 Hdctbl in first hdc, move marker up, hdctbl in each of next 22 (26, 30) hdc, (hdctbl-dec in next 2 hdc, hdctbl in each of next 23, (27, 31) hdc) 3 times, hdctbl-dec in last 2 hdc—96 (112, 128) hdc.

Rnd 4 Hdctbl in first hdc, move marker up, hdctbl in each of next 21 (25, 29) hdc, (hdctbl-dec in next 2 hdc, hdctbl in each of next 22 (26, 30) hdc) 3 times, hdctbl-dec in last 2 hdc—92 (108, 124) hdc.

Rnd 5 Hdctbl in first hdc, move marker up, hdctbl in each of next 20 (24, 28) hdc, (hdctbl-dec in next 2 hdc, hdctbl in each of next 21 (25, 29) hdc) 3 times, hdctbl-dec in last 2 hdc—88 (104, 120) hdc.

Rnd 6 Hdctbl in first hdc, move marker up, hdctbl in each of next 19 (23, 27) hdc, (hdctbl-dec in next 2 hdc, hdctbl in each of next 20 (24, 28) hdc) 3 times, hdctbl-dec in last 2 hdc—84 (100, 116) hdc.

Holding yarn together with one strand of elastic, work the last rounds even (without shaping).

Rnds 7–8 Hdctbl in first hdc, move marker up, hdctbl in each hdc around—84 (100, 116) hdc.

Rnd 9 Hdctbl in first hdc, move marker up, hdctbl in each hdc around to last hdc before marker, sc through the back loop only in last hdc, sl st in both loops of marked first hdc, fasten off.

Weave in ends, block skirt to finished measurements. ∎

(Stitch diagram and schematic on page 140.)

Sleeveless Tunic

Sleeveless Tunic

The subtle stripes that emerge from the variations in the *Taiyo Sock* yarn beautifully evoke the cool blues and warm sandy tones of the ocean.

Designed by Ann E. Smith

Skill Level: ■■■□

Materials

- 3 (4, 4, 5, 5) skeins 3½oz/100g skeins (each approx 462yd/422m) of Noro *Taiyo Sock* (cotton/wool/nylon/silk) in #8 teals/grey/khaki ①
- Size C/2 (2.75mm) crochet hook OR SIZE NEEDED TO OBTAIN GAUGE
- Size B/1 (2.25mm) crochet hook (for edging only)
- Stitch marker
- Yarn needle

Sizes

Instructions are written for size Small (Medium, Large, X-Large, and XX-Large; shown in size Small.

Finished Measurements

Bust 34 (38, 42, 46, 50)"/86.5 (96.5, 106.5, 117, 127)cm
Length 25½ (26, 26½, 27, 27½)"/65 (66, 67.5, 68.5, 70)cm

Gauge

21 sts and 25 rows to 4"/10cm over sc using C/2 (2.75mm) crochet hook. TAKE TIME TO CHECK GAUGE.

Stitch Glossary

FPdc (Front-post double crochet) Yarn over, insert hook from front to back and then to front again around post of indicated stitch, yarn over and draw up loop, [yarn over and draw through 2 loops on hook] twice.

sc2tog (single crochet 2 stitches together) [Insert hook in next stitch and draw up a loop] twice, yarn over and draw through all 3 loops on hook.

Back

With larger hook, ch 99 (109, 119, 129, 139).

Row 1 (WS) Sc in 2nd ch from hook and in next 40 (45, 50, 55, 60) ch, dc in next ch, sc in next 3 ch, dc in next 2 ch, sc in next 4 ch, dc in next 2 ch, sc in next 3 ch, dc in next ch, sc in each rem ch across—98 (108, 118, 128, 138) sts.

Row 2 (RS) Ch 1, turn, sc in first 41 (46, 51, 56, 61) sc, FPdc around next dc, sc in next 3 sc, FPdc around each of next 2 dc, sc in next 4 sc, FPdc around each of next 2 dc, sc in next 3 sc, FPdc around next dc, sc in each rem sc across.

Row 3 Ch 1, turn, sc in each sc across.

Begin post stitch pattern

Notes

1) The post stitch pattern can be worked by reading the written instructions below, or by following the chart.

2) The same number of sc stitches are worked at the beg and end of each row, centering the 30 post stitch pattern stitches.

3) If you choose to follow the chart, work each row as follows: Sc in the first 34 (39, 44, 49, 54) sts, work over the 30 center sts following the chart, then sc in the last 34 (39, 44, 49, 54) sts to the end of the row. You may wish to use markers on each side of the center 30 sts.

4) A stitch that is 2 rows below is in the row immediately beneath the row into which you would usually work. When working a post

stitch around a stitch 2 rows below, sk the corresponding stitch in the row into which you would usually work.

Row 1 (RS) Ch 1, turn, sc in first 34 (39, 44, 49, 54) sc, place marker in last sc made, sc in next 7 sc, FPdc around first FPdc 2 rows below, sc in next 3 sc, FPdc around each of next 2 FPdc 2 rows below, sc in next 4 sc, FPdc around each of next 2 FPdc 2 rows below, sc in next 3 sc, FPdc around next FPdc 2 rows below, sc in each rem st across. Move the marker up as work progresses.

Row 2 and all WS rows Ch 1, turn, sc in each sc across.

Row 3 Ch 1, turn, sc in each st up to and including marked st, sc in next 6 sc, FPdc around first FPdc 2 rows below, sc in next 3 sc, FPdc around next FPdc 2 rows below, sc in next sc, FPdc around next FPdc 2 rows below, sc in next 4 sc, FPdc around next FPdc 2 rows below, sc in next sc, FPdc around next FPdc 2 rows below, sc in next 3 sc, FPdc around next FPdc 2 rows below, sc in each rem st across.

Row 5 Ch 1, turn, sc in each st up to and including marked st, sc in next 5 sc, FPdc around first FPdc 2 rows below, sc in next 3 sc, FPdc around next FPdc 2 rows below, sc in next 2 sc, FPdc around next FPdc 2 rows below, sc in next 4 sc, FPdc around next FPdc 2 rows below, sc in next 2 sc, FPdc around next FPdc 2 rows below, sc in next 3 sc, FPdc around next FPdc 2 rows below, sc in each rem st across.

Row 7 Ch 1, turn, sc in each st up to and including marked st, sc in next 4 sc, [FPdc around first FPdc 2 rows below, sc in next 3 sc] twice, FPdc around next FPdc 2 rows below, sc in next 4 sc, FPdc around next FPdc 2 rows below, [sc in next 3 sc, FPdc around next FPdc 2 rows below] twice, sc in each rem st across.

Row 9 Ch 1, turn, sc in each st up to and including marked st, sc in next 3 sc, FPdc around first FPdc 2 rows below, sc in next 3 sc, [FPdc around next FPdc 2 rows below, sc in next 4 sc] 3 times, FPdc around next FPdc 2 rows below, sc in next 3 sc, FPdc around next FPdc 2 rows below, sc in each rem st across.

Row 11 Ch 1, turn, sc in each st up to and including marked st, sc in next 2 sc, FPdc around first FPdc 2 rows below, sc in next 3 sc, FPdc around next FPdc 2 rows below, sc in next 5 sc, FPdc around next FPdc 2 rows below, sc in next 4 sc, FPdc around next FPdc 2 rows below, sc in next 5 sc, FPdc around next FPdc 2 rows below, sc in next 3 sc, FPdc around next FPdc 2 rows below, sc in each rem st across.

Row 13 Ch 1, turn, sc in each st up to and including marked st, sc in next sc, FPdc around first FPdc 2 rows below, sc in next 3 sc, FPdc around next FPdc 2 rows below, sc in next 6 sc, FPdc around next FPdc 2 rows below, sc in next 4 sc, FPdc around next FPdc 2 rows below, sc in next 6 sc, FPdc around next FPdc 2 rows below, sc in next 3 sc, FPdc around next FPdc 2 rows below, sc in each rem st across.

Row 15 Ch 1, turn, sc in each st up to and including marked st, FPdc around first FPdc 2 rows below, sc in next 3 sc, FPdc around next FPdc 2 rows below, sc in next 7 sc, FPdc around next FPdc 2 rows below, sc in next 4 sc, FPdc around next FPdc 2 rows below, sc in next 7 sc, FPdc around next FPdc 2 rows below, sc in next 3 sc, FPdc around next FPdc 2 rows below, sc in each rem st across.

Row 17 Rep row 13.

Row 19 Rep row 11.

Row 21 Rep row 9.

Row 23 Rep row 7.

Row 25 Rep row 5.

Row 27 Rep row 3.

Row 29 Rep row 1.

Shape sides

Row 30 (WS; dec) Ch 1, turn, sc2tog, sc in each st across to last 2 sts, sc2tog—96 (106, 116, 126, 136) sts.

Continue in pattern as established for 14 rows.

Rep last 15 rows 4 more times—88 (98, 108, 118, 128) sts.

Work even in pattern as established until piece measures about 18"/45.5cm, end with a row 27 of the post stitch pattern.

Shape armholes

Row 1 (WS) Ch 1, turn, sl st in first 5 (6, 6, 8, 9) sts, sc in each sc across to last 5 (6, 6, 8, 9) sts; leave last 5 (6, 6, 8, 9) sts unworked—78 (86, 96, 102, 110) sts.

Row 2 (dec) Ch 1, turn, sc2tog, continue in pattern as established across to last 2 sts, sc2tog—76 (84, 94, 100, 108) sts.

Rep last row 6 (6, 8, 10, 12) more times—64 (72, 78, 80, 84) sts.

Work even in pattern as established until armhole measures about 7½ (8, 8¼, 9, 9½)"/19 (20.5, 21.5, 23, 24)cm, end with a RS row. Fasten off.

Front

Work same as back to armhole shaping. Ensure that the last row worked is a row 27 of post stitch pattern—88 (98, 108, 118, 128) sts.

Shape armhole and first side of neck

Row 1 (WS) Ch 1, turn, sl st in first 5 (6, 6, 8, 9) sts, sc in next 39 (43, 48, 51, 55) sts; leave rem sts unworked for second side—39 (43, 48, 51, 55) sts.

Row 2 Ch 1, turn, sc2tog, FPdc around each of next 2 FPdc 2 rows below, sc in next 3 sc, FPdc around next FPdc 2 rows below, sc in each sc across to last 2 sts, sc2tog—37 (41, 46, 49, 53) sts.

Row 3 Ch 1, turn, sc2tog, sc in each sc across—36 (40, 45, 48, 52) sts.

Row 4 Ch 1, turn, sc2tog, sc in next sc, FPdc around first FPdc 2 rows below, sc in next 3 sc, FPdc around next FPdc 2 rows below, sc in each sc across to last 2 sts, sc2tog—34 (38, 43, 46, 50) sts.

Rows 5–8 (8, 10, 12, 14) Rep last 2 rows 2 (2, 3, 4, 5) times—28 (32, 34, 34, 35) sts.

Next row (WS) Ch 1, turn, sc in each sc across.

Next row Ch 1, turn, sc2tog, sc in next sc, FPdc around first FPdc 2 rows below, sc in next 3 sc, FPdc around next FPdc 2 rows below, sc in each sc across—27 (31, 33, 33, 34) sts.

Rep last 2 rows 6 (8, 9, 9, 9) times—21 (23, 24, 24, 25) sts.

Next row (WS) Ch 1, turn, sc in each st across.

Next row Ch 1, turn, sc in first 2 sc, FPdc around first FPdc 2 rows below, sc in next 3 sc, FPdc around next FPdc 2 rows below, sc in each sc across.

Next row Ch 1, turn, sc in each sc across.

Next row Ch 1, turn, sc2tog, sc in next sc, FPdc around first FPdc 2 rows below, sc in next 3 sc, FPdc around next FPdc 2 rows below, sc in each sc across—20 (22, 23, 23, 24) sts.

Rep last 4 rows 5 more times—15 (17, 18, 18, 19) sts.

Work even in pattern as established until armhole measures same as back armhole. Fasten off.

Shape armhole and second side of neck

Row 1 (WS) With WS facing and larger hook, join yarn with sc in first unworked st following first side of neck, sc in each sc across to last 5 (6, 6, 8, 9) sts; leave rem sts unworked—39 (43, 48, 51, 55) sts.

Row 2 Ch 1, turn, sc2tog, sc in each sc across to last 8 sts, FPdc around first FPdc 2 rows below, sc in next 3 sc, FPdc around each of next 2 FPdc 2 rows below, sc2tog—37 (41, 46, 49, 53) sts.

Row 3 Ch 1, turn, sc in each sc across to last 2 sts, sc2tog—36 (40, 45, 48, 52) sts.

Row 4 Ch 1, turn, sc2tog, sc in each sc across to last 8 sts, FPdc around first FPdc 2 rows below, sc in next 3 sc, FPdc around next FPdc 2 rows below, sc in next sc, sc2tog—34 (38, 43, 46, 50) sts.

Rows 5–8 (8, 10, 12, 14) Rep last 2 rows 2 (2, 3, 4, 5) times—28 (32, 34, 34, 35) sts.

Next row (WS) Ch 1, turn, sc in each sc across.

Next row Ch 1, turn, sc in each sc across to last 8 sts, FPdc around first FPdc 2 rows below, sc in next 3 sc, FPdc around next FPdc 2 rows below, sc in next sc, sc2tog—27 (31, 33, 33, 34) sts.

Rep last 2 rows 6 (8, 9, 9, 9) times—21 (23, 24, 24, 25) sts.

Next row (WS) Ch 1, turn, sc in each st across.

Next row Ch 1, turn, sc in each sc across to last 7 sts, FPdc around first FPdc 2 rows below, sc in next 3 sc, FPdc around next FPdc 2 rows below, sc in last 2 sc.

Next row Ch 1, turn, sc in each sc across.

Next row Ch 1, turn, sc in each sc across to last 8 sts, FPdc around first FPdc 2 rows below, sc in next 3 sc, FPdc around next FPdc 2 rows below, sc in next sc, sc2tog—20 (22, 23, 23, 24) sts.

Rep last 4 rows 5 more times—15 (17, 18, 18, 19) sts.

Work even in pattern as established until armhole measures same as back armhole. Fasten off.

Finishing

Sew shoulder seams. Sew side seams.

Lower ric-rac edging

With RS facing and smaller hook, join yarn with sl st in lower edge at seam, working across opposite side of foundation ch, *ch 1, sl st in next ch; rep from * around. Fasten off.

Armhole edging

Rnd 1 With RS facing and smaller hook, join yarn with sc in armhole edge at underarm, work sc evenly spaced around armhole.

Rnd 2 Sl st in each sc around.

Rnd 3 Working below the sl sts of rnd 2 and into the sps between the sc sts of rnd 1, sl st in each sp around; join with sl st in first sl st. Fasten off.

Neck edging

With RS facing and smaller hook, join yarn with sl st in shoulder seam at beg of back neck edge.

Rnd 1 Sc evenly spaced all the way around neck edge, working sc3tog at center front V; join with sl st in first sc.

Rnd 2 Ch 1, sc in each sc around, working 3 decreases (sc2tog) evenly spaced across back neck and across each side of front neck (for a total of 9 decreases); join with sl st in first sc.

Rnd 3 (ric-rac edging) *Ch 1, sl st in next sc; rep from * around. Fasten off.

Weave in ends. ■

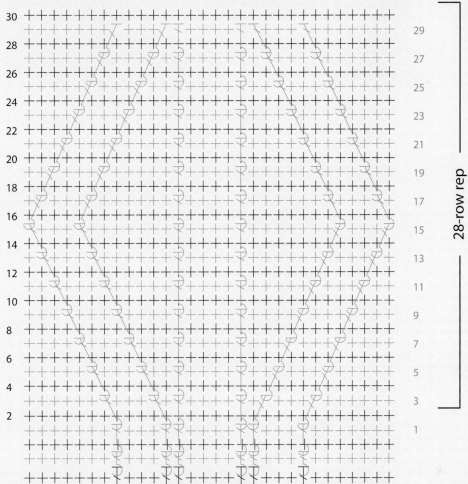

Post Stitch Pattern

28-row rep

Stitch Key

ch
sc
dc
FPdc

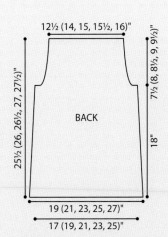

12½ (14, 15, 15½, 16)"

25½ (26, 26½, 27, 27½)"

7½ (8, 8½, 9, 9½)"

18"

BACK

19 (21, 23, 25, 27)"

17 (19, 21, 23, 25)"

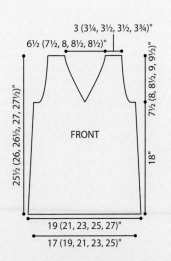

3 (3¼, 3½, 3½, 3¾)"

6½ (7½, 8, 8½, 8½)"

25½ (26, 26½, 27, 27½)"

7½ (8, 8½, 9, 9½)"

18"

FRONT

19 (21, 23, 25, 27)"

17 (19, 21, 23, 25)"

Bobbled Mitts

Bobbled Mitts

Rows of petite bobbles and ribbed cuffs add texture to these fetching fingerless mitts.

Designed by Karen Garlinghouse

Skill Level: ■■■☐

Materials

■ 2 1¾oz/50g skeins (each approx 137yd/125m) of Noro *Silk Garden Lite* (silk/mohair/lambswool) in #2036 fuschia/blues/greens ❸
■ Size G/6 (4mm) crochet hook OR SIZE TO OBTAIN GAUGE
■ Stitch marker

Size

Instructions are written for one size.

Finished Measurements

7"/18cm circumference x 7.5"/19cm long

Gauge

18 sts and 18 rows to 4"/10cm over pattern stitch using size G/7 (4.25mm) crochet hook. TAKE TIME TO CHECK GAUGE.

Stitch Glossary

Fsc (foundation single crochet) Ch 2, insert hook in 2nd ch from hook under top 2 strands, *yo, pull up a loop, yo, pull through first loop on hook (ch made), yo, pull through both loops on hook (1 Fsc made), insert hook in ch part (bottom) of st just made; rep from *.

FPdc (front post double crochet) Yo, insert hook around the post of the indicated st from the front, around the back and out to the front, yo and complete as for a regular dc. To keep st count correct, be careful to sk the st behind the FPdc.

Note

Join each rnd with a sl st.

Mitts

Fsc 32 sts. Join in a ring, pm at beg of rnd and move up with each rnd.

Rnds 1 and 2 Ch 1, sc in each st around—32 sc.

Rnd 3 Ch 1, *sc, FPdc in st 2 rows below; rep from * around—32 sts.

Rnds 4–6 Ch 1, *sc, FPdc in FPdc below; rep from * around—32 sts.

Rnds 7–8 Ch 1, sc in each st around—32 sc.

Rnd 9 Ch 1, *sc, tr; rep from * around.

Rnds 10–14 Rep rnd 1.

Rnd 15 Ch 1, *3 sc, tr; rep from * around.

Rnds 16–19 Rep rnd 1.

Rnd 20 Ch 1, 2 sc, *tr, 3 sc; rep from * around, end tr, sc.

Rnds 21–23 Rep rnd 1.

Thumb

Next rnd Ch 1, sc in first 4 sts of rnd, ch 8, sc in last 4 sts of rnd, join. Work on these 16 sts only.

Next rnd Ch 1, sc in next 4 sts, sc in each ch of ch-8, sc in next 4 sts—16 sc.

Cont in sc, dec 2 sts evenly on each of next 2 rnds—12 sc. Work even in sc for 3 rnds. Fasten off.

Hand

Rejoin yarn on opposite side (bottom of thumb) of ch-8.

Rnds 24–27 Work even in sc, placing 1 sc in each ch of ch-8 and each sc around—32 sc.

Rnd 28 Ch 1, sc, *tr, 3 sc; rep from * around, end tr, 2 sc.

Rnds 29–32 Work 4 rnds even in sc.

Rnd 33 Ch 1, *sc, tr; rep from * around.

Rnds 34–35 Work 2 rnds even in sc. Fasten off.

Finishing

Weave in ends. ■

Flower Motif Throw

Flower Motif Throw

A solid-colored mohair-blend accent yarn frames each flower motif (stitched in *Silk Garden Sock*) of this lovely afghan for a beautiful visual and tactile texture.

Designed by Yoko Hatta

Skill Level: ■■■□

Materials

■ 4 3½oz/100g skeins (each approx 328yd/300m) of Noro *Silk Garden Sock* (wool/silk/nylon/mohair) in #268 green/aqua/brown (MC) (2)
■ 2 .88oz/25g skeins (each approx 220yd/201m) of Debbie Bliss *Angel* (kid mohair/silk) in #08 denim (CC) (1)
■ Sizes B/1 (2.25mm) and C/2 (2.5mm) crochet hook
OR SIZE TO OBTAIN GAUGE

Finished Measurements

36"/91.5cm square

Note

Join motifs as work progresses following diagram. Join through ch-3 sp twice on each adjacent side as marked.

Gauge

Motif A measures 3½"/9cm in diameter using sizes B/1 (2.25mm)

and C/2 (2.5mm) crochet hooks and yarns as directed.
TAKE TIME TO CHECK GAUGE.

Stitch Glossary

2 dc cluster [Yo, insert hook in next st, yo and draw up a loop, yo, draw through 2 loops on hook] twice, yo and draw through all 3 loops on hook.
3 dc cluster [Yo, insert hook in next st, yo and draw up a loop, yo, draw through 2 loops on hook] 3 times, yo and draw through all 4 loops on hook.
Picot Ch 3, sl st in 3rd ch from hook.

Motif A (make 50)

With larger hook and MC, ch 5. Join in a ring.
Rnd 1 Ch 3 (counts as first dc), 2 dc cluster into ring, picot, *ch 5, 3 dc cluster, picot; rep from * a total of 5 times, ch 2, dc into beg cluster—6 clusters.
Rnd 2 Ch 1, sc in same ch-5 sp, ch 5, *(sc**, ch 5, sc) in next ch-5 sp, ch 5; rep from * around ending last rep at **, ch 2, dc in first sc of round—12 ch-5 loops
Rnd 3 Ch 1, *sc in ch-5 sp, ch 5; rep from * around, join with sl st to beg sc. Fasten off.
Rnd 4 With smaller hook and CC, join with sl st in any sc, ch 1, sc in same st, *work (3 sc, ch 3, 3 sc) in ch-5 sp; rep from * around, join to beg sc. Fasten off.

Motif B (make 50)

With larger hook and MC, ch 5. Join in a ring.
Rnd 1 Ch 3, picot, ch 3, (dc, picot, ch 3) in ring 5 times, sl st to 3rd ch to join—6 dc.
Rnd 2 Ch 1, *sc in ch-3 sp, ch 7; rep from * around, join to beg ch.
Rnd 3 Ch 1, *work (sc, hdc, 5 dc, hdc, sc) in ch-7 sp; rep from * around, join to beg sc.
Rnd 4 Sl st in each of next 2 sts, ch 1, *sc in first dc of shell, ch 5, sc in last dc of same shell, ch ch 5; rep from * around, join to beg sc. Fasten off.
Rnd 5 With smaller hook and CC, rep rnd 4 of Motif A.

Motif C (make 81)

With larger hook and MC, ch 5.
Rnd 1 Ch 4, sl st to join, ch 1, *sc in ring, picot, ch 3, sl st in ch-3 sp on motif A or B according to diagram, ch 3; rep from * a total of 4 times, join to beg sc—4 sc. Fasten off.

Finishing

Weave in ends. Block. ■

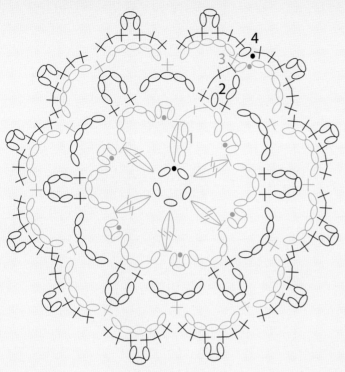

Motif A

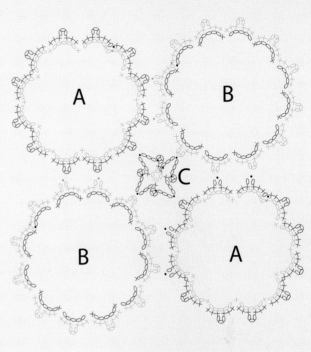

Joining Motifs

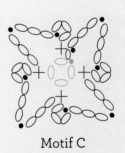

Motif C

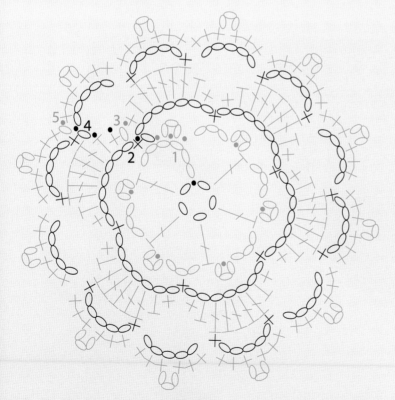

Motif B

Stitch Key

- • sl st
- ◯ ch
- + sc
- T hdc
- ⊤ dc

Swirl Tam

Swirl Tam

This cheerful topper features a subtle swirl pattern, and a vibrant *Silk Garden Sock* colorway creates a rainbow of stripes.

Designed by Dora Ohrenstein

Skill Level: ■■■□

Materials

- 1 3½oz/100g skein (each approx 328yd/300m) of Noro *Silk Garden Sock* (wool/silk/nylon/mohair) in #87 turquoise/pink/yellow (2)
- Size G/6 (4mm) crochet hook OR SIZE TO OBTAIN GAUGE
- Size E/4 (3.5mm) crochet hook (for band only)
- Yarn needle

Size

Instructions are written for one size. (For a smaller hat, about 9½"/24cm in diameter, work rnds 1–18, then rnds 21–26.)

Finished Measurements

Diameter (at widest point) approx 10½"/26.5cm
Circumference of band approx 17"/43cm (will stretch to fit a range of sizes)

Notes

1) Hat is worked in joined rounds with right side facing at all times.
2) The swirl is created by moving the post stitches one stitch over on each round.
3) A FPdc is worked around each FPdc of the previous round. To reach the FPdc of the previous round you will need to slant the hook backward slightly and in front of the last hdc made. On even rounds, a stitch is skipped "behind" each FPdc to keep the stitch count even. On increase rounds, hdc stitches are worked into *all* stitches of the previous rounds (including FPdc stitches and the stitches behind them).
4) Study the tops of stitches carefully so that the FPdc stitches line up in a spiral as desired. If you are right-handed, the top loops of a stitch appear slightly to the right of the post of the stitch. If you are left-handed, the top loops of a stitch appear slightly to the left of the post of the stitch.
5) If instructed to work in the first stitch, work into the same stitch in which the joining slip stitch was worked. If instructed to work into the next stitch, work into the stitch immediately following the stitch in which the joining slip stitch was worked. Only skip stitches when specifically instructed to do so. The beginning ch-2 counts as a hdc with its base in the same stitch in which the joining slip stitch was worked.

Gauge

20 sts and 11 rows to 4"/10cm over post stitch pattern using G/6 (4mm) crochet hook. TAKE TIME TO CHECK GAUGE.

Stitch Glossary

FPdc (Front-post double crochet) Yarn over, insert hook from front to back and then to front again around post of indicated stitch, yarn over and draw up loop, [yarn over and draw through 2 loops on hook] twice.
split-st (split stitch; worked over 2 sts) Yarn over, insert hook in same stitch as last stitch made (or last leg of last stitch made), draw

up a loop (3 loops on hook), yarn over, insert hook in next stitch and draw up a loop (5 loops on hook), yarn over and draw through 4 loops on hook, yarn over and draw through 2 loops on hook.

Tam

Beg at top of hat, with larger hook, make an adjustable ring.

Rnd 1 (RS) Ch 2 (counts as first hdc), work 13 hdc in ring; join with sl st in top of beg ch—14 hdc.

Rnd 2 Ch 2, FPdc around first hdc (beg ch is first hdc of previous round), *hdc in next hdc, FPdc around same hdc; rep from * around; join with sl st in top of beg ch—28 sts.

Rnd 3 Sl st in next st, ch 2, hdc in next st, FPdc around first FPdc of previous rnd, *hdc in next 2 sts, FPdc around next FPdc; rep from * around; join with sl st in top of beg ch—42 sts.

Rnd 4 Sl st in next st, ch 2, hdc in next 2 sts, FPdc around first FPdc of previous rnd, *hdc in next 3 sts, FPdc around next FPdc; rep from * around; join with sl st in top of beg ch—56 sts.

Rnd 5 Sl st in next st, ch 2, hdc in next 3 sts, FPdc around first FPdc of previous rnd, *hdc in next 4 sts, FPdc around next FPdc; rep from * around; join with sl st in top of beg ch—70 sts.

Rnds 6 and 7 Sl st in next 2 sts, ch 2, hdc in next 3 sts, FPdc around first FPdc of previous rnd, sk next st, *hdc in next 4 sts, FPdc around next FPdc, sk next st; rep from * around; join with sl st in top of beg ch—70 sts.

Rnd 8 Sl st in next st, ch 2, hdc in next 4 sts, FPdc around first FPdc of previous rnd, *hdc in next 5 sts, FPdc around next FPdc; rep from * around; join with sl st in top of beg ch—84 sts.

Rnd 9 Sl st in next st, ch 2, hdc in next 5 sts, FPdc around first FPdc of previous rnd, *hdc in next 6 sts, FPdc around next FPdc; rep from * around; join with sl st in top of beg ch—98 sts.

Rnd 10 Sl st in next st, ch 2, hdc in next 6 sts, FPdc around first FPdc of previous rnd, *hdc in next 7 sts, FPdc around next FPdc; rep from * around; join with sl st in top of beg ch—112 sts.

Rnd 11 Sl st in next st, ch 2, hdc in next 7 sts, FPdc around first FPdc of previous rnd, *hdc in next 8 sts, FPdc around next FPdc; rep from * around; join with sl st in top of beg ch—126 sts.

Rnd 12 Sl st in next st, ch 2, hdc in next 8 sts, FPdc around first FPdc of previous rnd, *hdc in next 9 sts, FPdc around next FPdc; rep from * around; join with sl st in top of beg ch—140 sts.

Rnd 13 Sl st in next st, ch 2, hdc in next 9 sts, FPdc around first FPdc of previous rnd, *hdc in next 10 sts, FPdc around next FPdc; rep from * around; join with sl st in top of beg ch—154 sts.

Rnds 14 and 15 Sl st in next 2 sts, ch 2, hdc in next 9 sts, FPdc around first FPdc of previous rnd, sk next st, *hdc in next 10 sts,

FPdc around next FPdc, sk next st; rep from * around; join with sl st in top of beg ch—154 sts.

Rnd 16 Sl st in next st, ch 2, hdc in next 10 sts, FPdc around first FPdc of previous rnd, *hdc in next 11 sts, FPdc around next FPdc; rep from * around; join with sl st in top of beg ch—168 sts.

Rnd 17 Sl st in next st, ch 2, hdc in next 11 sts, FPdc around first FPdc of previous rnd, *hdc in next 12 sts, FPdc around next FPdc; rep from * around; join with sl st in top of beg ch—182 sts.

Rnd 18 Sl st in next st, ch 2, hdc in next 12 sts, FPdc around first FPdc of previous rnd, *hdc in next 13 sts, FPdc around next FPdc; rep from * around; join with sl st in top of beg ch—196 sts.

Rnds 19 and 20 Sl st in next 2 sts, ch 2, hdc in next 12 sts, FPdc around first FPdc of previous rnd, sk next st, *hdc in next 13 sts, FPdc around next FPdc, sk next st; rep from * around; join with sl st in top of beg ch—196 sts. Do not fasten off.

Band

Change to smaller hook.

Rnd 21 Ch 1, sk first st, sc in next st, *sk next 2 sts, sc in next st; rep from * around to last 2 sts, sk last 2 sts; join with sl st in first sc—65 sts.

Rnd 22 Ch 1, sc in each sc around; join with sl st in first sc.

Rnd 23 Ch 3, beg in same st as join, split-st around; join with sl st in top of beg ch.

Rnds 24 and 25 Rep rnds 22 and 23.

Rnd 26 Ch 1, sc in each sc around; join with sl st in first sc. Fasten off.

Finishing

Weave in ends. ∎

Shell Scarf

Shell Scarf

A lacy shell motif worked in cool shades of blue, green, and violet creates an airy scarf that will be the focal point of your spring wardrobe.

Designed by Mary Jane Hall

Skill Level: ■■■□

Materials

■ 1 3½oz/100g skein (each approx 462yd/422m) of Noro *Taiyo Sock* (cotton/wool/nylon/silk) in #3 purples/blues (1)
■ Size F/5 (3.75mm) crochet hook OR SIZE TO OBTAIN GAUGE

Size

Instructions are written for one size.

Finished Measurements

6" x 70½"/15cm x 179cm (after blocking)

Gauge

2 shells + 2 sc and 8 rows to 4"/10cm over shell pat using size F/5 (3.75mm) crochet hook. TAKE TIME TO CHECK GAUGE.

Stitch Glossary

V-st Dc, ch 4, dc in same st.
Shell 4 dc, ch 2, 4 dc in same sp.

Scarf

Ch 43. **Row 1 (WS)** V-st in 13th ch from hook (counts as ch 5, dc, ch 4), ch 4, skip next 5 ch, dc in next ch,*ch 4, skip next 5 ch, V-st in next ch, ch 4, skip next 5 ch, dc in next ch; rep from * across, turn—10 dc (first dc is part of beg ch).
Row 2 (RS) Ch 5, (counts as dc, ch 2), sc in next ch-4 sp, *shell in next ch-4 sp, sc in next ch-4 sp **, ch 4, sc in next ch-4 sp; rep from * across, ending last rep at **, ch 2, dc in 3rd ch of t-ch, turn—3 shells.
Row 3 Ch 4 (counts as dc, ch 1), dc in first dc, skip next ch-2 sp, *ch 4, dc in next ch-2 sp in center of shell, ch 4 **, V-st in next ch-4 sp; rep from * across, ending last rep at **, (dc, ch 1, dc) in 3rd ch of t-ch, turn—11 dc.
Row 4 Ch 4 (counts as tr), 4 dc in next ch-1 sp, *sc in next ch-4 sp, ch 4, sc in next ch-4 sp**, shell in next ch-4 sp; rep from * across, ending last rep at **, 4 dc in next ch-1 sp of t-ch, tr in 3rd ch of t-ch, turn—2 full shells in center and half shell at each side; 3 ch-4 sp.
Row 5 Ch 7 (counts as dc, ch 4), *V-st in next ch-4 sp, ch 4**, dc in next ch-2 sp, ch 4; rep from * across, ending last rep at **, dc in 3rd ch of turning ch, turn—10 dc.
Rows 6–140 Rep rows 2–5. (**Note** If you wish to change the length of the scarf, end with a row 4.) Fasten off.

Shell edging

At opposite end of scarf, with WS facing, join yarn at end of starting chain.
Row 1 Ch 4 (counts as first dc, ch 1), dc in same sp, ch 2, sc in center of next sp, ch 2, *dc in base of V-st, ch 2, sc in next sp, V-st in next dc, sc in next sp, ch 2; rep from * across, ending with sc in last sp, ch 2, dc in 3rd ch of t-ch, turn
Row 2 Ch 4, (counts as tr), 4 dc in ch-2 sp, skip next ch 2, *sc in dc, ch 2, skip next ch 2, shell in next ch 4, ch 2, skip next ch 2; rep from * across, ending with sc in dc, skip next ch 2, dc in next ch 2, 4 dc in last ch-1 sp, tr in ch-3 of ch-4. Fasten off.

Finishing

Weave in ends. Block. ■

V-neck Pullover

V-neck Pullover

Take the plunge and stitch up this tunic-length sweater with a deep V neckline and cabled edgings. Worked in fiery red *Silk Garden*, it's a showstopper.

Designed by Mary Beth Temple

Skill Level: ■■■■

Materials

- 10 (12, 13, 15, 16) 1¾oz/50g skeins (each approx 110yd/100m) of Noro *Silk Garden* (silk/mohair/lambswool) in #84 reds (4)
- Size H/8 (5mm) crochet hook OR SIZE TO OBTAIN GAUGE
- Yarn needle

Sizes

Instructions are written for sizes Small (Medium, Large, X-Large, and XX-Large); shown in size Small.

Finished Measurements

Bust 36 (40, 44, 48, 52)"/91.5 (101.5, 111.5, 122, 132)cm
Waist 32 (36, 40, 44, 48)"/81 (91.5, 101.5, 112, 122)cm
Length 26 (26½, 27, 27¼, 28)"/66 (67.5, 68.5, 70, 71)cm

Gauge

12 sts and 10 rows = 4"/10cm over hdc using H/8 (5mm) crochet hook. TAKE TIME TO CHECK GAUGE.

Stitch Glossary

BPdc (Back-post double crochet) Yarn over, insert hook from back to front and then to back again around post of indicated stitch, yarn over and draw up loop, [yarn over and draw through 2 loops on hook] twice.
FPdc (Front-post double crochet) Yarn over, insert hook from front to back and then to front again around post of indicated stitch, yarn over and draw up loop, [yarn over and draw through 2 loops on hook] twice.
1/2 Left Cross (1 over 2 Left Cross) Skip next BPdc, FPdc around each of next 2 BPdc, working in front of 2 sts just made, FPdc around skipped BPdc.
hdc2tog (half double crochet 2 stitches together) [Yarn over, insert hook in next stitch and draw up a loop] twice, yarn over and draw through all 5 loops on hook.

Note

In this pattern hdc is treated like double crochet in that the turning chain is counted as a stitch, the first actual stitch of the row is skipped to keep the stitch count even and work into the turning chain as the last stitch of each row.

Front

Ch 55 (61, 67, 73, 79).
Row 1 (WS) Hdc in 3rd ch from hook (beg ch counts as hdc), hdc in each rem ch across—54 (60, 66, 72, 78) sts.
Row 2 (RS) Ch 2 (counts as hdc here and throughout), turn, FPdc around each of next 3 sts, hdc in each st across to last 4 sts, FPdc around each of next 3 sts, hdc in last st (the t-ch).
Row 3 Ch 2, turn, BPdc around each of next 3 sts, hdc in each st across to last 4 sts, BPdc around each of next 3 sts, hdc in last st.

Row 4 Ch 2, turn, 1/2 Left Cross, hdc in each st across to last 4 sts, 1/2 Left Cross, hdc in last st.

Rep last 2 rows until piece measures 8"/20.5cm from beg, end with a WS row (Row 3).

Next 2 rows Ch 2, turn, hdc in each st across.

Shape waist

Row 1 (RS; dec) Ch 2, turn, hdc2tog, hdc in each st across to last 3 sts, hdc2tog, hdc in last st—52 (58, 64, 70, 76) sts.

Row 2 Ch 2, turn, hdc in each st across.

Rows 3–6 Rep last 2 rows 2 times—48 (54, 60, 66, 72) sts.

Row 7 (inc) Ch 2, turn, 2 hdc in next st, hdc in each st across to last 2 sts, 2 hdc in next st, hdc in last st—50 (56, 62, 68, 74) sts.

Row 8 Ch 2, turn, hdc in each st across.

Rows 9–12 Rep last 2 rows 2 times—54 (60, 66, 72, 78) sts.

Row 13 Ch 2, turn, hdc in each st across.

Rep last row until piece measures 13"/33cm from beg, end with a WS row.

Begin neck

Row 1 (RS) Ch 2, turn, hdc in next 22 (25, 28, 31, 34) sts, FPdc around each of next 3 sts, hdc in next 2 sts, FPdc around each of next 3 sts, hdc in each rem st across.

Row 2 Ch 2, turn, hdc in next 22 (25, 28, 31, 34) sts, BPdc around each of next 3 sts, hdc in next 2 sts, BPdc around each of next 3 sts, hdc in each rem st across.

Row 3 Ch 2, turn, hdc in next 22 (25, 28, 31, 34) sts, 1/2 Left Cross, hdc in next 2 sts, 1/2 Left Cross, hdc in each rem st across.

Row 4 Rep row 2.

Shape first side of neck

Row 1 (RS) Ch 2, turn, hdc in next 20 (23, 26, 29, 32) sts, hdc2tog, 1/2 Left Cross, hdc in next st; leave rem sts unworked—26 (29, 32, 35, 38) sts.

Row 2 Ch 2, turn, BPdc around each of next 3 sts, hdc in each rem st across.

Row 3 (dec) Ch 2, turn, hdc in each st to 2 sts before next post st, hdc2tog, 1/2 Left Cross, hdc in last st—25 (28, 31, 34, 37) sts.

Row 4 Rep row 2.

Rep last 2 rows 2 more times—23 (26, 29, 32, 35) sts.

Note Piece should measure about 18"/45.5cm from beg.

Shape armhole

Row 1 (RS) Ch 1, turn, sl st in first 4 (5, 6, 7, 8) sts, ch 2 (counts as first hdc with base in same st as last sl st made), hdc in each st across to 2 sts before next post st, hdc2tog, 1/2 Left Cross, hdc in last st—19 (21, 23, 25, 27) sts.

Row 2 Ch 2, turn, BPdc around each of next 3 sts, hdc in each rem st across.

Row 3 Ch 2, turn, hdc2tog, hdc in each st across to 2 sts before next post st, hdc2tog, 1/2 Left Cross, hdc in last st—17 (19, 21, 23, 25) sts.

Row 4 Rep row 2.

Rep last 2 rows 0 (1, 1, 2, 2) times—17 (17, 19, 19, 21) sts.

Next row Ch 2, turn, hdc in each st across to 2 sts before next post st, hdc2tog, 1/2 Left Cross, hdc in last st—16 (16, 18, 18, 20) sts.

Next row Rep row 2.

Rep last 2 rows until 12 (13, 14, 15, 16) sts rem.

Work even in pattern as established until armhole measures 8 (8½, 9, 9½, 10)"/20.5 (21.5, 23, 24, 25.5)". Fasten off.

Shape second side of neck

Row 1 (RS) With RS facing, join yarn with sl st in first unworked st following first side of neck, ch 2, 1/2 Left Cross, hdc2tog, hdc in each rem st across—26 (29, 32, 35, 38) sts.

Row 2 Ch 2, turn, hdc in each st to next post st, BPdc around each of next 3 sts, hdc in last st.

Row 3 (decrease) Ch 2, turn, 1/2 Left Cross, hdc2tog, hdc in each rem st across—25 (28, 31, 34, 37) sts.

Row 4 Rep row 2.

Rep last 2 rows 2 more times—23 (26, 29, 32, 35) sts.

Note Piece should measure about 18"/45.5cm from beg.

Shape armhole

Row 1 (RS) Ch 2, turn, 1/2 Left Cross, hdc2tog, hdc in each st across to last 3 (4, 5, 6, 7) sts; leave rem sts unworked for armhole—19 (21, 23, 25, 27) sts.

Row 2 Ch 2, turn, hdc in each st to next post st, BPdc around each of next 3 sts, hdc in last st.

Row 3 Ch 2, turn, 1/2 Left Cross, hdc2tog, hdc in each st across to last 3 sts, hdc2tog, hdc in last st—17 (19, 21, 23, 25) sts.

Row 4 Rep row 2.

Rep last 2 rows 0 (1, 1, 2, 2) times—17 (17, 19, 19, 21) sts.

Next row Ch 2, turn, 1/2 Left Cross, hdc2tog, hdc in each rem st across—16 (16, 18, 18, 20) sts.

Next row Rep row 2.

Rep last 2 rows until 12 (13, 14, 15, 16) sts rem.

Work even in pattern as established until armhole measures 8 (8½, 9, 9½, 10)"/20.5 (21.5, 23, 24, 25.5)". Fasten off.

Back

Work same as front through waist shaping—54 (60, 66, 72, 78) sts.

Next row Ch 2, turn, hdc in each st across.

Rep last row until piece measures 18"/45.5cm from beg, end with a WS row.

Shape armholes

Row 1 (RS) Ch 1, turn, sl st in first 4 (5, 6, 7, 8) sts, ch 2 (counts as first hdc with base in same st as last sl st made), hdc in each st across to last 3 (4, 5, 6, 7) sts; leave rem sts unworked—48 (52, 56, 60, 64) sts.

Row 2 Ch 2, turn, hdc in each st across.

Row 3 Ch 2, turn, hdc2tog, hdc in each st across to last 3 sts, hdc2tog, hdc in last st—46 (50, 54, 58, 62) sts.

Rep last 2 rows 0 (1, 1, 2, 2) times—46 (48, 52, 54, 58) sts.

Row 4 Rep row 2.

Rep last row until piece has 2 fewer rows than front, end with a WS row.

Shape first side of neck

Row 1 (RS) Ch 2, turn, hdc in next 11 (12, 13, 14, 15) sts, hdc2tog; leave rem sts unworked for neck and second side of neck—13 (14, 15, 16, 17) sts.

Row 2 Ch 2, turn, hdc2tog, hdc in each rem st across—12 (13, 14, 15, 16) sts. Fasten off.

Shape second side of neck

Row 1 (RS) With RS facing, sk next 18 (18, 20, 20, 22) unworked sts following first side of neck, join yarn with sl st in next st, ch 2 (counts as hdc with base in same st as joining sl st), hdc2tog, hdc in each rem st across—13 (14, 15, 16, 17) sts.

Row 2 Ch 2, turn, hdc in each st across to last 2 sts, hdc2tog—12 (13, 14, 15, 16) sts. Fasten off.

Sleeves (make 2)

Ch 31 (33, 35, 37, 39).

Row 1 Hdc in 3rd ch from hook (beg ch counts as first hdc), hdc in each rem ch across—30 (32, 34, 36, 38) hdc.

Rows 2–4 Ch 2, turn, hdc in each hdc across.

Row 5 (inc) Ch 2, turn, hdc in first st (increase made), hdc in each st across to last st, 2 hdc in last st—32 (34, 36, 38, 40) hdc.

Next 5 (4, 3, 3, 3) rows Ch 2, turn, hdc in each st across.

Rep last 6 (5, 4, 4, 4) rows 5 (6, 7, 8, 9) times—42 (46, 50, 54, 58) hdc.

Rep row 2 until piece measures 16 (16¼, 17, 17½, 18)"/40.5 (42, 43, 44.5, 45.5)cm from beg.

Shape sleeve cap

Row 1 Ch 1, turn, sl st in first 4 (5, 6, 7, 8) sts, ch 2, hdc in each hdc across to last 3 (4, 5, 6, 7) sts; leave rem sts unworked—36 (38, 40, 42, 44) hdc.

Row 2 Ch 2, turn, hdc in each st across.

Next 4 (5, 6, 7, 8) rows Ch 2, turn, hdc2tog, hdc in each st across to last 3 sts, hdc2tog, hdc in last st—28 hdc.

Next 3 rows Rep row 2.

Next 3 rows Ch 2, turn, hdc2tog, hdc in each st across to last 3 sts, hdc2tog, hdc in last st—22 hdc.

Next row Ch 1, turn, sl st in first st, sc in next st, hdc in each st across to last 2 sts, sc in next st; leave last st unworked—20 sts (not counting first sl st).

Next row Ch 1, turn, sl st in first 3 sts, sc in next st, hdc in each st across to last 4 sts, sc in next st; leave rem sts unworked—14 sts (not counting beg sl sts). Fasten off.

Sleeve trim (make 2)

Ch 6.

Row 1 Hdc in 3rd ch from hook (beg ch counts as first hdc), hdc in each rem ch across—5 hdc.

Row 2 (RS) Ch 2, turn, FPdc around each of next 3 sts, hdc in last st.

Row 3 Ch 2, turn, BPdc around each of next 3 sts, hdc in last st.

Row 4 Ch 2, turn, 1/2 Left Cross, hdc in last st.

Rep last 2 rows until piece measures long enough to go around wrist-edge of sleeve. Fasten off.

Finishing

Sew shoulder seams.

Hold RS of one sleeve trim piece and wrist edge of one sleeve together. From WS and working through both thicknesses, join yarn with sc in corner, sc evenly spaced across to join sleeve trim to wrist edge of sleeve. Rep to attach other sleeve trim piece to wrist edge of other sleeve.

Sew sleeves into armholes.

Sew side and sleeve seams, leaving 8"/20.5cm of lower side seam open for side slits.

Lower edging

With RS facing, join yarn with sl st in lower edge at center back, ch 1, rev sc evenly spaced all the way around the lower edge, including side slits; join with sl st in beg ch.

Neck edging

With RS facing, join yarn with sl st in center back neck edge, ch 1, rev sc evenly spaced around neck edge; join with sl st in beg ch.

Cuff edging

With RS facing, join yarn with sl st in sleeve seam, ch 1, rev sc evenly spaced around wrist edge; join with sl st in beg ch. Rep around other wrist edge.

Weave in ends. ∎

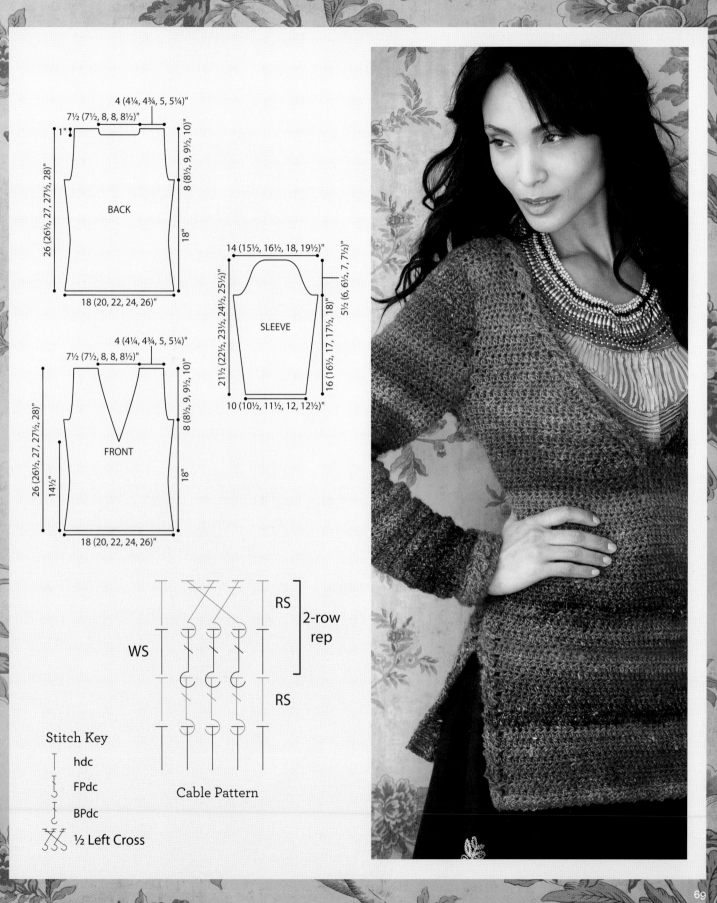

4 (4¼, 4¾, 5, 5¼)"

7½ (7½, 8, 8, 8½)"

1"

8 (8½, 9, 9½, 10)"

BACK

26 (26½, 27, 27½, 28)"

18"

18 (20, 22, 24, 26)"

14 (15½, 16½, 18, 19½)"

5½ (6, 6½, 7, 7½)"

SLEEVE

21½ (22½, 23½, 24½, 25½)"

16 (16½, 17, 17½, 18)"

10 (10½, 11½, 12, 12½)"

4 (4¼, 4¾, 5, 5¼)"

7½ (7½, 8, 8, 8½)"

8 (8½, 9, 9½, 10)"

FRONT

26 (26½, 27, 27½, 28)"

14½"

18"

18 (20, 22, 24, 26)"

RS

2-row rep

WS

RS

Cable Pattern

Stitch Key

| hdc

FPdc

BPdc

½ Left Cross

Bobbled Hat

Bobbled Hat

Treble crochet stitches pepper the surface of this gorgeously textured hat, giving the appearance of hundreds of tiny bobbles.

Designed by Linda Permann

Skill Level: ■■■□

Materials

- 2 1¾oz/50g skeins (each approx 110yd/100m) of Noro *Silk Garden* (silk/mohair/lambswool) in #341 plum/mustard/tomato/tangerine 〔3〕
- Size 7 (4.5mm) crochet hook OR SIZE TO OBTAIN GAUGE

Sizes

Instructions are written for size Small. Changes for sizes Medium and Large are in parentheses. (Shown in size Medium.)

Finished Measurements

Circumference 17 (20, 23)"/43 (51, 58.5)cm
Length 7½ (8¼ 9½)"/19 (21.5, 24)cm

Gauge

14 sts and 12 rows to 4"/10cm over pattern stitch using size 7 (4.5mm) crochet hook. TAKE TIME TO CHECK GAUGE.

Notes

1) It might be helpful to place a marker in the first sc of each round, for ease of finding both the end of the round and also the stitch into which to place the joining sl st.
2) Tr's should pop out to the RS. Sometimes they need a little push to help them. It is easier to do this as you work, rather than all at the end.
3) The top of the hat might begin to ruffle. This will work itself out when the sides of the hat are added.

Hat

Make an adjustable ring.

Rnd 1 (RS) Ch 1, [sc, tr] 5 times in ring, join with sl st in first sc—5 sc, 5 tr.

Rnd 2 Ch 1, [sc tr] in each st around; join with sl st in first sc—10 sc, 10 tr.

Rnd 3 Ch 1, sc in first st, [tr, sc] in next st, tr in next st, [sc, tr] in next st, *sc in next st, [tr, sc] in next st, tr in next st, [sc, tr] in next st; rep from * around, join with sl st in first sc—15 sc, 15 tr.

Rnd 4 Ch 1, sc in first st, tr in next st, [sc, tr] in next st, *sc in next st, tr in next st, [sc, tr] in next st, rep from * around; join with sl st in first sc—20 sc, 20 tr.

Rnd 5 Ch 1, sc in first st, tr in next st, sc in next st, [tr, sc] in next st, tr in next st, sc in next st, tr in next st, [sc, tr] in next st, *sc in next st, tr in next st, sc in next st, [tr, sc] in next st, tr in next st, sc in next st, tr in next st, [sc, tr] in next st; rep from * around, join with sl st in first sc—25 sc, 25 tr.

Rnd 6 Ch 1, sc in first st, tr in next st, sc in next st, tr in next st, [sc, tr] in next st, *[sc in next st, tr in next st] twice, [sc, tr] in next st; rep from * around, join with sl st in first sc—30 sc, 30 tr.

Sizes M (L) only

Rnd 7 Ch 1, sc in first st, [tr in next st, sc in next st] twice, [tr, sc] in next st, tr in next st, [sc in next st, tr in next st] twice, [sc, tr] in next st, *sc in next st, [tr in next st, sc in next st] twice, [tr, sc] in next st, tr in next st, [sc in next st, tr in next st] twice, [sc, tr] in next st; rep from * around, join with sl st in first sc—35 sc, 35 tr.

Size L only

Rnd 8 Ch 1, sc in first st, tr in next st, [sc in next st, tr in next st] twice, [sc, tr] in next st, *[sc in next st, tr in next st] 3 times, [sc, tr] in next st; rep from * around, join with sl st in first sc—40 sc, 40 tr.

All sizes

Rnd 1 Ch 4 (counts as tr), sc in next tr, *tr in next sc, sc in next tr; rep from * around, join with sl st in first sc—35 (40, 45) sc, 35 (40, 45) tr.

Rnd 2 Ch 1, sc in first tr, tr in next sc, *sc in next tr, tr in next sc; rep from * around, join with sl st in first sc.

Rnds 3–14 (16, 18) Rep rnds 1 and 2. Do not fasten off.

Brim

Note Brim is worked in ribbing from side to side along lower edge of hat.

Row 1 (RS) Ch 8, sc in 2nd ch from hook and each ch across—7 sc.

Row 2 Sl st in next 2 sts along brim of hat, turn, sc in each sc across—7 sc.

Row 3 Ch 1, turn, sc in back loop only of each sc across.

Row 4 Rep row 2.

Rows 5–60 (70, 80) Rep rows 3 and 4 twenty-eight (thirty-three, thirty-eight) times.

Fasten off, leaving a long tail for sewing.

Finishing

Using tail, whipstitch first and last row of brim tog from WS. Weave in ends. Wet-block for best results. ∎

Short-Row Scarf

Short-Row Scarf

Short-row shaping lends this simple-looking scarf subtle shifts in color. A muted colorway of *Silk Garden* adds to the mystery.

Designed by Wilhelmine Peers

Skill Level: ■■■□

Materials
- 4 1¾oz/50g skein (each approx 110yd/100m) of Noro *Silk Garden* (silk/mohair/lambswool) in #252 black/turquoise/green (4)
- Size I/9 (5.5mm) crochet hook OR SIZE TO OBTAIN GAUGE
- Yarn needle

Size
Instructions are written for one size.

Finished Measurements
Approx 9"/23cm wide x 50"/127cm long

Note
There are a number of ways to crochet short rows. The method used in this scarf produces shallow triangles, without leaving abrupt edges at the end of short rows.

Gauge
15 sts and 16 rows to 4"/10cm over sc using I/9 (5.5mm) crochet hook. TAKE TIME TO CHECK GAUGE.

Stitch Glossary
sc2tog (single crochet 2 stitches together) [Insert hook in next stitch and draw up a loop] twice, yarn over and draw through all 3 loops on hook.

Scarf
Ch 36.
Row 1 (RS) Sc in 2nd ch from hook and in each ch across—35 sc.
Short row triangle
Row 2 Ch 1, turn, sc in each sc across to last 4 sc, sc2tog; leave last 2 sc unworked—32 sc.
Row 3 Ch 1, turn, sk the sc2tog, sl st in next st, sc in each sc across—30 sc.
Row 4 Ch 1, turn, sc in each sc across to last 4 sts (the last 4 sts are 3 sc and one sl st), sc2tog; leave last sc and sl st unworked—28 sc.
Row 5 Ch 1, turn, sk the sc2tog, sl st in next st, sc in each sc across—26 sc.
Rows 6–17 Rep last 2 rows 6 times, leaving 2 more sts (one sc and one sl st) unworked at the end of each even-numbered row—2 sc rem.
Row 18 Ch 1, turn, work 35 sc evenly spaced all the way across the piece, this can be accomplished by working one sc in each sc, sl st, ch-1, and side of each sc2tog—35 sc.
Rep rows 2–18, until almost all yarn has been used or scarf has reached desired length.
Notes Each repeat of rows 2–18 will create another short row triangle. Every other triangle slants in the opposite direction. Fasten off.

Finishing
Weave in ends. Steam block to soften fabric, and shape scarf into a consistent rectangle. ■

(Stitch diagram on page 140.)

Lacy Capelet

Lacy Capelet

This elegant capelet crocheted in shades of ecru, mocha, and gray features a subtle stitch pattern inspired by the shape of a pineapple.

Designed by Yoko Hatta

Skill Level: ■■■■

Materials

- 3 skeins 3½oz/100g skeins (each approx 328yd/300m) of Noro *Silk Garden Sock* (wool/silk/nylon/mohair) in #269 crème/tan/grey **2**
- Size E/4 (3.5mm) crochet hook OR SIZE TO OBTAIN GAUGE
- Yarn needle

Size

Instructions are written for one size.

Finished Measurements

Capelet measures approx 18"/45.5cm long x 28"/71cm in circumference at top x 62"/157.5cm in circumference at lower edge.

Note

Capelet is worked from neck edge down. The number of stitches in each pineapple increases gradually to create the flared shape.

Gauge

2 pattern repeats = 4¾"/12cm over pineapple pattern at top edge, and 9½ rows to 4"/10cm over entire pineapple pattern using E/4 (3.5mm) crochet hook. TAKE TIME TO CHECK GAUGE.

Stitch Glossary

picot Ch 4, sl st in 3rd ch from hook, ch 1.
picot-shell (2 dc, picot, 2 dc) in indicated space.
shell (2 dc, ch 2, 2 dc) in indicated stitch or space.
wide-picot Ch 5, sl st in 3rd ch from hook, ch 2.

Capelet

Ch 168; taking care not to twist ch, join with sl st in first ch to form a ring.
Rnd 1 (RS) Ch 3 (counts as first dc here and throughout), (dc, ch 2, 2 dc) in same ch as joining sl st, *ch 2, sk next 3 ch, sc in next ch, [ch 3, sk next ch, sc in next ch] 3 times, ch 2, sk next 3 ch, (2 dc, [ch 2, 2 dc] twice) in next ch; rep from * 10 more times (to last 13 ch), ch 2, sk next 3 ch, sc in next ch, [ch 3, sk next ch, sc in next ch] 3 times, ch 2, sk last 3 ch, 2 dc again in same ch as beg, ch 2; join with sl st in top of beg ch—12 pattern repeats.
Rnd 2 (WS) Turn, sl st in first ch-2 sp, ch 5 (counts as dc, ch 2 here and throughout), 2 dc in same ch-2 sp, ch 2, sk next ch-2 sp, sc in next ch-3 sp, [ch 3, sc in next ch-3 sp] twice, ch 2, sk next ch-2 sp, shell in next ch-2 sp, *ch 2, shell in next ch-2 sp, ch 2, sk next ch-2 sp, sc in next ch-3 sp, [ch 3, sc in next ch-3 sp] twice, ch 2, sk next ch-2 sp, shell in next ch-2 sp; rep from * around, ch 2, dc in same ch-2 sp as beg; join with sl st in 3rd ch of beg ch.
Rnd 3 Sl st in next ch-2 sp (formed by turning ch), turn, ch 3, dc in same ch-2 sp, ch 1, (dc, ch 1, dc) in next ch-2 sp, ch 1, shell in next ch-2 sp, ch 2, sk next ch-2 sp, sc in next ch-3 sp, ch 3, sc in next ch-3 sp, *ch 2, sk next ch-2 sp, shell in next ch-2 sp, ch 1, (dc, ch 1, dc) in next ch-2 sp, ch 1, shell in next ch-2 sp, ch 2, sk next ch-2 sp, sc in next ch-3 sp, ch 3, sc in next ch-3 sp; rep from * around to last ch-2

sp, ch 2, sk last ch-2 sp, 2 dc in same ch-2 sp as beg, ch 2; join with sl st in top of beg ch.

Rnd 4 Turn, (sl st, ch 5, 2 dc) in first ch-2 sp, ch 2, sk next ch-2 sp, sc in next ch-3 sp, ch 2, sk next ch-2 sp, shell in next ch-2 sp, ch 1, sk next ch-1 sp, 5 dc in next ch-1 sp, *ch 1, sk next ch-1 sp, shell in next ch-2 sp, ch 2, sk next ch-2 sp, sc in next ch-3 sp, ch 2, sk next ch-2 sp, shell in next ch-2 sp, ch 1, sk next ch-1 sp, 5 dc in next ch-1 sp; rep from * around to last ch-1 sp, ch 1, sk last ch-1 sp, dc in same ch-2 sp as beg; join with sl st in 3rd ch of beg ch.

Rnd 5 Sl st in next ch-2 sp, turn, ch 3, dc in same ch-2 sp, ch 2, sk next ch-1 sp, dc in next dc, [ch 1, dc in next dc] 4 times, ch 2, sk next ch-1 sp, shell in next ch-2 sp, *sk next 2 ch-2 sps, shell in next ch-2 sp, ch 2, sk next ch-1 sp, dc in next dc, [ch 1, dc in next dc] 4 times, ch 2, sk next ch-1 sp, shell in next ch-2 sp; rep from * around to last 2 ch-2 sps, sk last 2 ch-2 sps, 2 dc in same ch-2 sp as beg, ch 2; join with sl st in top of beg ch.

Rnd 6 Turn, (sl st, ch 5, 2 dc) in first ch-2 sp, ch 1, shell in next ch-2 sp, ch 2, sk next ch-2 sp, sc in next ch-1 sp, [ch 3, sc in next ch-1 sp] 3 times, *ch 2, sk next ch-2 sp, shell in next ch-2 sp, ch 1, shell in next ch-2 sp, ch 2, sk next ch-2 sp, sc in next ch-1 sp, [ch 3, sc in next ch-1 sp] 3 times; rep from * around to last ch-2 sp, ch 2, sk last ch-2 sp, dc in same ch-2 sp as beg; join with sl st in 3rd ch of beg ch.

Rnd 7 Sl st in next ch-2 sp, turn, ch 3, dc in same ch-2 sp, ch 2, sk next ch-2 sp, sc in next ch-3 sp, [ch 3, sc in next ch-3 sp] twice, ch 2, sk next ch-2 sp, shell in next ch-2 sp, ch 2, dc in next ch-1 sp, *ch 2, shell in next ch-2 sp, ch 2, sk next ch-2 sp, sc in next ch-3 sp, [ch 3, sc in next ch-3 sp] twice, ch 2, sk next ch-2 sp, shell in next ch-2 sp, ch 2, dc in next ch-1 sp; rep from * around, ch 2, 2 dc in same ch-2 sp as beg, ch 2; join with sl st in top of beg ch.

Rnd 8 Turn, (sl st, ch 5, 2 dc) in first ch-2 sp, ch 2, sk next ch-2 sp, (dc, ch 2, dc) in next dc, ch 2, sk next ch-2 sp, shell in next ch-2 sp, ch 2, sk next ch-2 sp, sc in next ch-3 sp, ch 3, sc in next ch-3 sp, *ch 2, sk next ch-2 sp, shell in next ch-2 sp, ch 2, sk next ch-2 sp, (dc, ch 2, dc) in next dc, ch 2, sk next ch-2 sp, shell in next ch-2 sp, ch 2, sk next ch-2 sp, sc in next ch-3 sp, ch 3, sc in next ch-3 sp; rep from * around to last ch-2 sp, ch 2, sk last ch-2 sp, dc in same ch-2 sp as beg; join with sl st in 3rd ch of beg ch.

Rnd 9 Sl st in next ch-2 sp, turn, ch 3, dc in same ch-2 sp, ch 2, sk next ch-2 sp, sc in next ch-3 sp, ch 2, sk next ch-2 sp, shell in next ch-2 sp, ch 1, sk next ch-2 sp, 7 dc in next ch-2 sp, *ch 1, sk next ch-2 sp, shell in next ch-2 sp, ch 2, sk next ch-2 sp, sc in next ch-3 sp, ch 2, sk next ch-2 sp, shell in next ch-2 sp, ch 1, sk next ch-2 sp, 7 dc in next ch-2 sp; rep from * around to last ch-2 sp, ch 1, sk last ch-2 sp, 2 dc in same ch-2 sp as beg, ch 2; join with sl st in top of beg ch.

Rnd 10 Turn, (sl st, ch 5, 2 dc) in first ch-2 sp, ch 2, sk next ch-1 sp, dc in next dc, [ch 1, dc in next dc] 6 times, ch 2, sk next ch-1 sp, shell in next ch-2 sp, *sk next 2 ch-2 sps, shell in next ch-2 sp, ch 2, sk next ch-1 sp, dc in next dc, [ch 1, dc in next dc] 6 times, ch 2, sk next ch-1 sp, shell in next ch-2 sp; rep from * around to last 2 ch-2 sps, sk last 2 ch-2 sps, dc in same ch-2 sp as beg; join with sl st in 3rd ch of beg ch.

Rnd 11 Sl st in next ch-2 sp, turn, ch 3, dc in same ch-2 sp, ch 1, shell in next ch-2 sp, ch 3, sk next ch-2 sp, sc in next ch-1 sp, [ch 3, sc in next ch-1 sp] 5 times, *ch 3, sk next ch-2 sp, shell in next ch-2 sp, ch 1, shell in next ch-2 sp, ch 3, sk next ch-2 sp, sc in next ch-1 sp, [ch 3, sc in next ch-1 sp] 5 times; rep from * around to last ch-2 sp, ch 3, sk last ch-2 sp, 2 dc in same ch-2 sp as beg, ch 2; join with sl st in top of beg ch.

Rnd 12 Turn, (sl st, ch 5, 2 dc) in first ch-2 sp, ch 3, sk next ch-3 sp, sc in next ch-3 sp, [ch 3, sc in next ch-3 sp] 4 times, ch 3, sk next ch-3 sp, shell in next ch-2 sp, *ch 2, sk next ch-1 sp, shell in next ch-2 sp, ch 3, sk next ch-3 sp, sc in next ch-3 sp, [ch 3, sc in next ch-3 sp] 4 times, ch 3, sk next ch-3 sp, shell in next ch-2 sp; rep from * around to last ch-1 sp, ch 2, sk last ch-1 sp, dc in same ch-2 sp as beg; join with sl st in 3rd ch of beg ch.

Rnd 13 Sl st in next ch-2 sp, turn, ch 3, dc in same ch-2 sp, ch 2, dc in next ch-2 sp, ch 2, shell in next ch-2 sp, ch 3, sk next ch-3 sp, sc in next ch-3 sp, [ch 3, sc in next ch-3 sp] 3 times, *ch 3, sk next ch-3 sp, shell in next ch-2 sp, ch 2, dc in next ch-2 sp, ch 2, shell in next ch-2 sp, ch 3, sk next ch-3 sp, sc in next ch-3 sp, [ch 3, sc in next ch-3 sp] 3 times; rep from * around to last ch-3 sp, ch 3, sk last ch-3 sp, 2 dc in same ch-2 sp as beg, ch 2; join with sl st in top of beg ch.

Rnd 14 Turn, (sl st, ch 5, 2 dc) in first ch-2 sp, ch 3, sk next ch-3 sp, sc in next ch-3 sp, [ch 3, sc in next ch-3 sp] twice, ch 3, sk next ch-3 sp, shell in next ch-2 sp, ch 2, sk next ch-2 sp, (dc, ch 3, dc) in next dc, *ch 2, sk next ch-2 sp, shell in next ch-2 sp, ch 3, sk next ch-3 sp, sc in next ch-3 sp, [ch 3, sc in next ch-3 sp] twice, ch 3, sk next ch-3 sp, shell in next ch-2 sp, ch 2, sk next ch-2 sp, (dc, ch 3, dc) in next dc; rep from * around to last ch-2 sp, ch 2, sk last ch-2 sp, dc in same ch-2 sp as beg; join with sl st in 3rd ch of beg ch.

Rnd 15 Sl st in next ch-2 sp, turn, ch 3, dc in same ch-2 sp, ch 2, sk next ch-2 sp, 9 dc in next ch-3 sp, ch 2, sk next ch-2 sp, shell in next ch-2 sp, ch 3, sk next ch-3 sp, sc in next ch-3 sp, ch 3, sc in next ch-3 sp, *ch 3, sk next ch-3 sp, shell in next ch-2 sp, ch 2, sk next ch-2 sp, 9 dc in next ch-3 sp, ch 2, sk next ch-2 sp, shell in next ch-2 sp, ch 3, sk next ch-3 sp, sc in next ch-3 sp, ch 3, sc in next ch-3 sp; rep from * around to last ch-3 sp, ch 3, sk last ch-3 sp, 2 dc in same ch-2 sp as beg, ch 2; join with sl st in top of beg ch.

Rnd 16 Turn, (sl st, ch 5, 2 dc) in first ch-2 sp, ch 3, sk next ch-3 sp, sc in next ch-3 sp, ch 3, sk next ch-3 sp, shell in next ch-2 sp, ch 2, sk next ch-2 sp, dc in next dc, [ch 1, dc in next dc] 8 times, *ch 2, sk next ch-2 sp, shell in next ch-2 sp, ch 3, sk next ch-3 sp, sc in next ch-3 sp, ch 3, sk next ch-3 sp, shell in next ch-2 sp, ch 2, sk next ch-2 sp, dc in next dc, [ch 1, dc in next dc] 8 times; rep from * around to last ch-2 sp, ch 2, sk last ch-2 sp, dc in same ch-2 sp as beg; join with sl st in 3rd ch of beg ch.

Rnd 17 Sl st in next ch-2 sp, turn, ch 3, dc in same ch-2 sp, ch 3, sk next ch-2 sp, sc in next ch-1 sp, [ch 3, sc in next ch-1 sp] 7 times, ch 3, sk next ch-2 sp, shell in next ch-2 sp, *sk next 2 ch-3 sps, shell in next ch-2 sp, ch 3, sk next ch-2 sp, sc in next ch-1 sp, [ch 3, sc in next ch-1 sp] 7 times, ch 3, sk next ch-2 sp, shell in next ch-2 sp; rep from * around to last 2 ch-3 sps, sk last 2 ch-3 sps, 2 dc in same ch-2 sp as beg, ch 2; join with sl st in top of beg ch.

Rnd 18 Turn, (sl st, ch 5, 2 dc) in first ch-2 sp, ch 1, shell in next ch-2 sp, ch 3, sk next ch-3 sp, sc in next ch-3 sp, [ch 3, sc in next ch-3 sp] 6 times, *ch 3, sk next ch-3 sp, shell in next ch-2 sp, ch 1, shell in next ch-2 sp, ch 3, sk next ch-3 sp, sc in next ch-3 sp, [ch 3, sc in next ch-3 sp] 6 times; rep from * around to last ch-3 sp, ch 3, sk last ch-3 sp, dc in same ch-2 sp as beg; join with sl st in 3rd ch of beg ch.

Rnd 19 Sl st in next ch-2 sp, turn, ch 3, dc in same ch-2 sp, ch 3, sk next ch-3 sp, sc in next ch-3 sp, [ch 3, sc in next ch-3 sp] 5 times, ch 3, sk next ch-3 sp, shell in next ch-2 sp, *ch 2, sk next ch-1 sp, shell in next ch-2 sp, ch 3, sk next ch-3 sp, sc in next ch-3 sp, [ch 3, sc in next ch-3 sp] 5 times, ch 3, sk next ch-3 sp, shell in next ch-2 sp; rep from * around to last ch-1 sp, ch 2, sk last ch-1 sp, 2 dc in same ch-2 sp as beg, ch 2; join with sl st in top of beg ch.

Rnd 20 Turn, (sl st, ch 5, 2 dc) in first ch-2 sp, ch 2, dc in next ch-2 sp, ch 2, shell in next ch-2 sp, ch 3, sk next ch-3 sp, sc in next ch-3 sp, [ch 3, sc in next ch-3 sp] 4 times, *ch 3, sk next ch-3 sp, shell in next ch-2 sp, ch 2, dc in next ch-2 sp, ch 2, shell in next ch-2 sp, ch 3, sk next ch-3 sp, sc in next ch-3 sp, [ch 3, sc in next ch-3 sp] 4 times; rep from * around to last ch-3 sp, ch 3, sk last ch-3 sp, dc in same ch-2 sp as beg; join with sl st in 3rd ch of beg ch.

Rnd 21 Sl st in next ch-2 sp, turn, ch 3, dc in same ch-2 sp, ch 3, sk next ch-3 sp, sc in next ch-3 sp, [ch 3, sc in next ch-3 sp] 3 times, ch 3, sk next ch-3 sp, shell in next ch-2 sp, ch 2, sk next ch-2 sp, (dc, ch 5, dc) in next dc, *ch 2, sk next ch-2 sp, shell in next ch-2 sp, ch 3, sk next ch-3 sp, sc in next ch-3 sp, [ch 3, sc in next ch-3 sp] 3 times, ch 3, sk next ch-3 sp, shell in next ch-2 sp, ch 2, sk next ch-2 sp, (dc, ch 5, dc) in next dc; rep from * around to last ch-2 sp, ch 2, sk last ch-2 sp, 2 dc in same ch-2 sp as beg, ch 2; join with sl st in top of beg ch.

Rnd 22 Turn, (sl st, ch 5, 2 dc) in first ch-2 sp, ch 2, sk next ch-2 sp, 10 dc in next ch-5 sp, ch 2, sk next ch-2 sp, shell in next ch-2 sp, ch 3, sk next ch-3 sp, sc in next ch-3 sp, [ch 3, sc in next ch-3 sp] twice, *ch 3, sk next ch-3 sp, shell in next ch-2 sp, ch 2, sk next ch-2 sp, 10 dc in next ch-5 sp, ch 2, sk next ch-2 sp, shell in next ch-2 sp, ch 3, sk next

ch-3 sp, sc in next ch-3 sp, [ch 3, sc in next ch-3 sp] twice; rep from * around to last ch-3 sp, ch 3, sk last ch-3 sp, dc in same ch-2 sp as beg; join with sl st in 3rd ch of beg ch.

Rnd 23 Sl st in next ch-2 sp, turn, ch 3, dc in same ch-2 sp, ch 3, sk next ch-3 sp, sc in next ch-3 sp, ch 3, sc in next ch-3 sp, ch 3, sk next ch-3 sp, shell in next ch-2 sp, ch 2, sk next ch-2 sp, dc in next dc, [ch 1, dc in next dc] 9 times, *ch 2, sk next ch-2 sp, shell in next ch-2 sp, ch 3, sk next ch-3 sp, sc in next ch-3 sp, ch 3, sc in next ch-3 sp, ch 3, sk next ch-3 sp, shell in next ch-2 sp, ch 2, sk next ch-2 sp, dc in next dc, [ch 1, dc in next dc] 9 times; rep from * around to last ch-2 sp, ch 2, sk last ch-2 sp, 2 dc in same ch-2 sp as beg, ch 2; join with sl st in top of beg ch.

Rnd 24 Turn, (sl st, ch 5, 2 dc) in first ch-2 sp, ch 3, sk next ch-2 sp, sc in next ch-1 sp, [ch 3, sc in next ch-1 sp] 8 times, ch 3, sk next ch-2 sp, shell in next ch-2 sp, ch 3, sk next ch-3 sp, sc in next ch-3 sp, *ch 3, sk next ch-3 sp, shell in next ch-2 sp, ch 3, sk next ch-2 sp, sc in next ch-1 sp, [ch 3, sc in next ch-1 sp] 8 times, ch 3, sk next ch-2 sp, shell in next ch-2 sp, ch 3, sk next ch-3 sp, sc in next ch-3 sp; rep from * around to last ch-3 sp, ch 3, sk last ch-3 sp, dc in same ch-2 sp as beg; join with sl st in 3rd ch of beg ch.

Rnd 25 Sl st in next ch-2 sp, turn, ch 3, dc in same ch-2 sp, sk next 2 ch-3 sps, shell in next ch-2 sp, ch 3, sk next ch-3 sp, sc in next ch-3 sp, [ch 3, sc in next ch-3 sp] 7 times, *ch 3, sk next ch-3 sp, shell in next ch-2 sp, sk next 2 ch-3 sps, shell in next ch-2 sp, ch 3, sk next ch-3 sp, sc in next ch-3 sp, [ch 3, sc in next ch-3 sp] 7 times; rep from * around to last ch-3 sp, ch 3, sk last ch-3 sp, 2 dc in same ch-2 sp as beg, ch 2; join with sl st in top of beg ch.

Rnd 26 Turn, (sl st, ch 5, 2 dc) in first ch-2 sp, ch 3, sk next ch-3 sp, sc in next ch-3 sp, [ch 3, sc in next ch-3 sp] 6 times, ch 3, sk next ch-3 sp, shell in next ch-2 sp, *ch 1, shell in next ch-2 sp, ch 3, sk next ch-3 sp, sc in next ch-3 sp, [ch 3, sc in next ch-3 sp] 6 times, ch 3, sk next ch-3 sp, shell in next ch-2 sp; rep from * around, ch 1, dc in same ch-2 sp as beg; join with sl st in 3rd ch of beg ch.

Rnd 27 Sl st in next ch-2 sp, turn, ch 3, dc in same ch-2 sp, ch 2, sk next ch-1 sp, shell in next ch-2 sp, ch 3, sk next ch-3 sp, sc in next ch-3 sp, [ch 3, sc in next ch-3 sp] 5 times, *ch 3, sk next ch-3 sp, shell in next ch-2 sp, ch 2, sk next ch-1 sp, shell in next ch-2 sp, ch 3, sk next ch-3 sp, sc in next ch-3 sp, [ch 3, sc in next ch-3 sp] 5 times; rep from * around to last ch-3 sp, ch 3, sk last ch-3 sp, 2 dc in same ch-2 sp as beg, ch 2; join with sl st in top of beg ch.

Rnd 28 Turn, (sl st, ch 5, 2 dc) in first ch-2 sp, ch 3, sk next ch-3 sp, sc in next ch-3 sp, [ch 3, sc in next ch-3 sp] 4 times, ch 3, sk next ch-3 sp, shell in next ch-2 sp, *ch 2, dc in next ch-2 sp, ch 2, shell in next ch-2 sp, ch 3, sk next ch-3 sp, sc in next ch-3 sp, [ch 3, sc in next ch-3 sp] 4 times, ch 3, sk next ch-3 sp, shell in next ch-2 sp; rep from * around to last ch-2 sp, ch 2, dc in last ch-2 sp, ch 2, dc in same ch-2 sp as beg; join with sl st in 3rd ch of beg ch.

Rnd 29 Sl st in next ch-2 sp, turn, ch 3, dc in same ch-2 sp, ch 2, sk next ch-2 sp, (dc, ch 5, dc) in next dc, ch 2, sk next ch-2 sp, shell in next ch-2 sp, ch 3, sk next ch-3 sp, sc in next ch-3 sp, [ch 3, sc in next ch-3 sp] 3 times, *ch 3, sk next ch-3 sp, shell in next ch-2 sp, ch 2, sk next ch-2 sp, (dc, ch 5, dc) in next dc, ch 2, sk next ch-2 sp, shell in next ch-2 sp, ch 3, sk next ch-3 sp, sc in next ch-3 sp, [ch 3, sc in next ch-3 sp] 3 times; rep from * around to last ch-3 sp, ch 3, sk last ch-3 sp, 2 dc in same ch-2 sp as beg, ch 2; join with sl st in top of beg ch.

Rnd 30 Turn, (sl st, ch 5, 2 dc) in first ch-2 sp, ch 3, sk next ch-3 sp, sc in next ch-3 sp, [ch 3, sc in next ch-3 sp] twice, ch 3, sk next ch-3 sp, shell in next ch-2 sp, ch 2, sk next ch-2 sp, 11 dc in next ch-5 sp, *ch 2, sk next ch-2 sp, shell in next ch-2 sp, ch 3, sk next ch-3 sp, sc in next ch-3 sp, [ch 3, sc in next ch-3 sp] twice, ch 3, sk next ch-3 sp, shell in next ch-2 sp, ch 2, sk next ch-2 sp, 11 dc in next ch-5 sp; rep from * around to last ch-2 sp, ch 2, dc in same ch-2 sp as beg; join with sl st in 3rd ch of beg ch.

Rnd 31 Sl st in next ch-2 sp, turn, ch 3, dc in same ch-2 sp, ch 2, sk next ch-2 sp, dc in next dc, [ch 1, dc in next dc] 10 times, ch 2, sk next ch-2 sp, shell in next ch-2 sp, ch 3, sk next ch-3 sp, sc in next ch-3 sp, ch 3, sc in next ch-3 sp, *ch 3, sk next ch-3 sp, shell in next ch-2 sp, ch 2, sk next ch-2 sp, dc in next dc, [ch 1, dc in next dc] 10 times, ch 2, sk next ch-2 sp, shell in next ch-2 sp, ch 3, sk next ch-3 sp, sc in next ch-3 sp, ch 3, sc in next ch-3 sp; rep from * around to last ch-3 sp, ch 3, sk last ch-3 sp, 2 dc in same ch-2 sp as beg, ch 2; join with sl st in top of beg ch.

Rnd 32 Turn, (sl st, ch 5, 2 dc) in first ch-2 sp, ch 3, sk next ch-3 sp, sc in next ch-3 sp, ch 3, sk next ch-3 sp, shell in next ch-2 sp, ch 3, sk next ch-2 sp, sc in next ch-1 sp, [ch 3, sc in next ch-1 sp] 9 times, *ch 3, sk next ch-2 sp, shell in next ch-2 sp, ch 3, sk next ch-3 sp, sc in next ch-3 sp, ch 3, sk next ch-3 sp, shell in next ch-2 sp, ch 3, sk next ch-2 sp, sc in next ch-1 sp, [ch 3, sc in next ch-1 sp] 9 times; rep from * around to last ch-2 sp, ch 3, sk last ch-2 sp, dc in same ch-2 sp as beg; join with sl st in 3rd ch of beg ch.

Rnd 33 Sl st in next ch-2 sp, turn, ch 3, dc in same ch-2 sp, ch 3, sk next ch-3 sp, sc in next ch-3 sp, [ch 3, sc in next ch-3 sp] 8 times, ch 3, sk next ch-3 sp, shell in next ch-2 sp, *sk next 2 ch-3 sps, shell in next ch-2 sp, ch 3, sk next ch-3 sp, sc in next ch-3 sp, [ch 3, sc in next ch-3 sp] 8 times, ch 3, sk next ch-3 sp, shell in next ch-2 sp; rep from * around to last 2 ch-3 sps, sk last 2 ch-3 sps, 2 dc in same ch-2 sp as beg, ch 2; join with sl st in top of beg ch.

Rnd 34 Turn, (sl st, ch 5, 2 dc) in first ch-2 sp, ch 1, shell in next ch-2 sp, ch 3, sk next ch-3 sp, sc in next ch-3 sp, [ch 3, sc in next ch-3 sp] 7 times, *ch 3, sk next ch-3 sp, shell in next ch-2 sp, ch 1, shell in next ch-2 sp, ch 3, sk next ch-3 sp, sc in next ch-3 sp, [ch 3, sc in next ch-3

sp] 7 times; rep from * around to last ch-3 sp, ch 3, sk last ch-3 sp, dc in same ch-2 sp as beg; join with sl st in 3rd ch of beg ch.

Rnd 35 Sl st in next ch-2 sp, turn, ch 3, dc in same ch-2 sp, ch 3, sk next ch-3 sp, sc in next ch-3 sp, [ch 3, sc in next ch-3 sp] 6 times, ch 3, sk next ch-3 sp, shell in next ch-2 sp, *ch 2, sk next ch-1 sp, shell in next ch-2 sp, ch 3, sk next ch-3 sp, sc in next ch-3 sp, [ch 3, sc in next ch-3 sp] 6 times, ch 3, sk next ch-3 sp, shell in next ch-2 sp; rep from * around to last ch-1 sp, ch 2, sk last ch-1 sp, 2 dc in same ch-2 sp as beg, ch 2; join with sl st in top of beg ch.

Rnd 36 Turn, (sl st, ch 5, 2 dc) in first ch-2 sp, ch 2, dc in next ch-2 sp, ch 2, shell in next ch-2 sp, ch 3, sk next ch-3 sp, sc in next ch-3 sp, [ch 3, sc in next ch-3 sp] 5 times, *ch 3, sk next ch-3 sp, shell in next ch-2 sp, ch 2, dc in next ch-2 sp, ch 2, shell in next ch-2 sp, ch 3, sk next ch-3 sp, sc in next ch-3 sp, [ch 3, sc in next ch-3 sp] 5 times; rep from * around to last ch-3 sp, ch 3, sk last ch-3 sp, dc in same ch-2 sp as beg; join with sl st in 3rd ch of beg ch.

Rnd 37 Sl st in next ch-2 sp, turn, ch 3, dc in same ch-2 sp, ch 3, sk next ch-3 sp, sc in next ch-3 sp, [ch 3, sc in next ch-3 sp] 4 times, ch 3, sk next ch-3 sp, shell in next ch-2 sp, ch 2, sk next ch-2 sp, (dc, ch 5, dc) in next dc, *ch 2, sk next ch-2 sp, shell in next ch-2 sp, ch 3, sk next ch-3 sp, sc in next ch-3 sp, [ch 3, sc in next ch-3 sp] 4 times, ch 3, sk next ch-3 sp, shell in next ch-2 sp, ch 2, sk next ch-2 sp, (dc, ch 5, dc) in next dc; rep from * around to last ch-2 sp, ch 2, sk last ch-2 sp, 2 dc in same ch-2 sp as beg, ch 2; join with sl st in top of beg ch.

Rnd 38 Turn, (sl st, ch 5, 2 dc) in first ch-2 sp, ch 2, sk next ch-2 sp, 12 dc in next ch-5 sp, ch 2, sk next ch-2 sp, shell in next ch-2 sp, ch 3, sk next ch-3 sp, sc in next ch-3 sp, [ch 3, sc in next ch-3 sp] 3 times, *ch 3, sk next ch-3 sp, shell in next ch-2 sp, ch 2, sk next ch-2 sp, 12 dc in next ch-5 sp, ch 2, sk next ch-2 sp, shell in next ch-2 sp, ch 3, sk next ch-3 sp, sc in next ch-3 sp, [ch 3, sc in next ch-3 sp] 3 times; rep from * around to last ch-3 sp, ch 3, sk last ch-3 sp, dc in same ch-2 sp as beg; join with sl st in 3rd ch of beg ch.

Rnd 39 Sl st in next ch-2 sp, turn, ch 3, dc in same ch-2 sp, ch 3, sk next ch-3 sp, sc in next ch-3 sp, [ch 3, sc in next ch-3 sp] twice, ch 3, sk next ch-3 sp, shell in next ch-2 sp, ch 2, sk next ch-2 sp, dc in next dc, [ch 1, dc in next dc] 11 times, *ch 2, sk next ch-2 sp, shell in next ch-2 sp, ch 3, sk next ch-3 sp, sc in next ch-3 sp, [ch 3, sc in next ch-3 sp] twice, ch 3, sk next ch-3 sp, shell in next ch-2 sp, ch 2, sk next ch-2 sp, dc in next dc, [ch 1, dc in next dc] 11 times; rep from * around to last ch-2 sp, ch 2, sk last ch-2 sp, 2 dc in same ch-2 sp as beg, ch 2; join with sl st in top of beg ch.

Rnd 40 Turn, (sl st, ch 5, 2 dc) in first ch-2 sp, ch 3, sk next ch-2 sp, sc in next ch-1 sp, [ch 3, sc in next ch-1 sp] 10 times, ch 3, sk next ch-2 sp, shell in next ch-2 sp, ch 3, sk next ch-3 sp, sc in next ch-3 sp, ch 3, sc in next ch-3 sp, *ch 3, sk next ch-3 sp, shell in next ch-2 sp, ch 3, sk next ch-2 sp, sc in next ch-1 sp, [ch 3, sc in next ch-1 sp] 10 times, ch 3, sk next ch-2 sp, shell in next ch-2 sp, ch 3, sk next ch-3 sp, sc in next ch-3 sp, ch 3, sc in next ch-3 sp; rep from * around to last ch-3 sp, ch 3, sk last ch-3 sp, dc in same ch-2 sp as beg; join with sl st in 3rd ch of beg ch.

Rnd 41 Sl st in next ch-2 sp, turn, ch 3, dc in same ch-2 sp, ch 3, sk next ch-3 sp, sc in next ch-3 sp, ch 3, sk next ch-3 sp, shell in next z ch-2 sp, ch 3, sk next ch-3 sp, sc in next ch-3 sp, [ch 3, sc in next ch-3 sp] 9 times, *ch 3, sk next ch-3 sp, shell in next ch-2 sp, ch 3, sk next ch-3 sp, sc in next ch-3 sp, ch 3, sk next ch-3 sp, shell in next ch-2 sp, ch 3, sk next ch-3 sp, sc in next ch-3 sp, [ch 3, sc in next ch-3 sp] 9 times; rep from * around to last ch-3 sp, ch 3, sk last ch-3 sp, 2 dc in same ch-2 sp as beg, ch 2; join with sl st in top of beg ch.

Rnd 42 Turn, (sl st, ch 5, 2 dc) in first ch-2 sp, ch 3, sk next ch-3 sp, sc in next ch-3 sp, [ch 3, sc in next ch-3 sp] 8 times, ch 3, sk next ch-3 sp, shell in next ch-2 sp, *sk next 2 ch-3 sps, shell in next ch-2 sp, ch 3, sk next ch-3 sp, sc in next ch-3 sp, [ch 3, sc in next ch-3 sp] 8 times, ch 3, sk next ch-3 sp, shell in next ch-2 sp; rep from * around to last 2 ch-3 sps, sk last 2 ch-3 sps, dc in same ch-2 sp as beg; join with sl st in 3rd ch of beg ch.

Rnd 43 Sl st in next ch-2 sp, turn, ch 3, dc in same ch-2 sp, picot-shell in next ch-2 sp, picot, sk next ch-3 sp, sc in next ch-3 sp, [wide-picot, sc in next ch-3 sp] 7 times, *wide-picot, sk next ch-3 sp, picot-shell in each of next 2 ch-2 sps, wide-picot, sk next ch-3 sp, sc in next ch-3 sp, [wide-picot, sc in next ch-3 sp] 7 times; rep from * around to last ch-3 sp, wide-picot, sk last ch-3 sp, 2 dc in same ch-2 sp as beg, picot; join with sl st in top of beg ch. Fasten off.

Finishing
Neck edging
Rnd 1 (RS) With RS facing, working across opposite side of foundation ch, join yarn with sc in ch at base of any (2 dc, ch 2, 2 dc, ch 2, 2 dc), ch 3, sk next 3 ch, sc in next ch, [ch 3, sk next 2 ch, sc in next ch] twice, *ch 3, sk next 3 ch, sc in next ch (at base of next shell), ch 3, sk next 3 ch, sc in next ch, [ch 3, sk next 2 ch, sc in next ch] twice; rep from * around to last 3 ch, sk last 3 ch; join with ch 1, hdc in first sc (join counts as ch-3 sp)—48 ch-3 sps.

Rnd 2 Ch 1, sc in first ch-3 sp (formed by join), ch 3, sl st in sc just made, *ch 3, sc in next ch-3 sp, ch 3, sl st in sc just made; rep from * around, ch 3, join with sl st in first sc.

Fasten off. Weave in ends. ∎

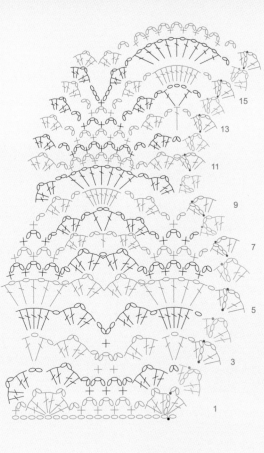

17
15
13
11
9
7
5
3
1

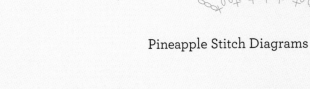

43
41
39
37
35

33
31
29
27
25
23
21
19

Stitch Key

- ◯ ch
- • sl st
- + sc
- ⊤ hdc
- ⊤ dc

Edging Diagram

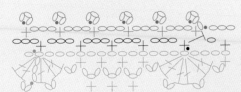

2
1

Nesting Bowls

Nesting Bowls

As pretty as they are practical, these colorful bowls will brighten your tabletop while wrangling your clutter.

Designed by Jacqueline van Dillen

Skill Level: ■■□□

Materials

- 2 3½oz/100g skeins (each approx 220yd/201m) of Noro *Taiyo* (cotton/silk/wool/nylon) in #17 orange/red/grey 〔4〕
- Size G/7 (4.5mm) crochet hook
OR SIZE TO OBTAIN GAUGE
- 4 stitch markers (for Medium and Large bowls only, optional)
- Yarn needle

Sizes

Instructions are written for size Small. Changes for Medium and Large are in parentheses.

Finished Measurements

Circumference 4¾ (6, 7)"/12 (15, 18)cm
Height 4 (4½, 5½)"/10 (11.5, 14)cm

Notes

1) One bowl can be made with a single skein of *Taiyo*.
2) Small and Medium bowls have wrong side of stitches on outside of bowl. Large bowl has right side of stitches on outside of bowl, for a slightly different look.
3) Stitch markers are used to indicate increase locations in the last rounds of the Medium and Large bowls. If you can "read" your stitches, you may not need to use the markers.

Gauge

20 sts and 21 rounds to 4"/10cm over sc worked in rounds using G/7 (4.5mm) crochet hook. TAKE TIME TO CHECK GAUGE.

Stitch Glossary

FPsc (Front-post single crochet) Insert hook from front to back and then to front again around post of indicated stitch, yarn over and draw up loop, yarn over and draw through 2 loops on hook.
sc2tog (single crochet 2 stitches together) [Insert hook in next stitch and draw up a loop] twice, yarn over and draw through all 3 loops on hook.

Small Bowl

Beg at bottom of bowl, ch 4; join with sl st in first ch to form ring.
Rnd 1 (RS) Work 8 sc in ring; join with sl st in first sc—8 sc.
Note Work first stitch of each round in same stitch as joining slip stitch. Do not turn, unless otherwise instructed.
Rnd 2 Ch 1, 2 sc in each sc around; join with sl st in first sc—16 sc.
Rnd 3 Ch 1, [sc in next sc, 2 sc in next sc] 8 times; join with sl st in first sc—24 sc.
Rnd 4 Ch 1, [sc in next 2 sc, 2 sc in next sc] 8 times; join with sl st in first sc—32 sc.
Rnd 5 Ch 1, [sc in next 3 sc, 2 sc in next sc] 8 times; join with sl st in first sc—40 sc.
Rnd 6 Ch 1, [sc in next 4 sc, 2 sc in next sc] 8 times; join with sl st in first sc—48 sc.
Rnd 7 Ch 1, [sc in next 5 sc, 2 sc in next sc] 8 times; join with sl st in first sc—56 sc.
Rnd 8 Ch 1, [sc in next 6 sc, 2 sc in next sc] 8 times; join with sl st in

first sc—64 sc.

Rnd 9 Ch 1, [sc in next 7 sc, 2 sc in next sc] 8 times; join with sl st in first sc—72 sc.

Rnd 10 Ch 1, [sc in next 17 sc, 2 sc in next sc] 4 times; join with sl st in first sc—76 sc.

Bottom ridge (WS) Ch 1, turn, FPsc around each sc; join with sl st in first sc.

Shape sides

Rnd 11 (RS) Ch 1, turn, working into tops of sts of rnd 10, sc in each sc around; join with sl st in first sc.

Note A decrease (sc2tog) is worked in every other round, to shape sides. Place the decrease randomly within each decrease round. For best results, place the decrease at a different location in each decrease round.

Rnd 12 (decrease) Ch 1, sc in each sc around, working one sc2tog to decrease 1 st anywhere in rnd; join with sl st in first sc—75 sc.

Rnd 13 Ch 1, sc in each sc around; join with sl st in first sc.

Rnds 14–19 Rep last 2 rnds 3 times—72 sc at the end of rnd 19.

Rnd 20 Ch 1, sc in each sc around; join with sl st in first sc. Rep last rnd until bowl is desired height.

Scallop edging

Ch 3 (counts as dc), 2 dc in same sc as join, *sk next 2 sc, sc in next sc, sk next 2 sc, 6 dc in next sc; rep from * around to last 5 sc, sk next 2 sc, sc in next sc, sk last 2 sc, 3 dc in same sc as beg; join with sl st in top of beg ch—12 scallops. Fasten off.

Medium Bowl

Work same as Small bowl through rnd 9—72 sc.

Rnd 10 Ch 1, [sc in next 17 sc, 2 sc in next sc, place marker in last sc made] 4 times; join with sl st in first sc—76 sc.

Rnds 11–13 Ch 1, [sc in each sc to marked sc, 2 sc in marked sc, move marker to last sc made] 4 times; join with sl st in first sc—88 sc at the end of rnd 13.

Bottom ridge (WS) Ch 1, turn, FPsc around each sc; join with sl st in first sc.

Shape sides

Rnd 14 (RS) Ch 1, turn, working into tops of sts of rnd 13, sc in each sc around; join with sl st in first sc.

Note Two decreases (sc2tog) are worked in every other round, to shape sides. Place the decreases randomly within each decrease round. For best results, place the decreases at different locations in each decrease round.

Rnd 15 (decrease) Ch 1, sc in each sc around working two sc2tog to decrease 2 sts anywhere in rnd; join with sl st in first sc—86 sc.

Rnd 16 Ch 1, sc in each sc around; join with sl st in first sc.

Rnds 17–24 Rep last 2 rnds 4 times—78 sc at the end of rnd 24.

Rnd 25 Ch 1, sc in each sc around; join with sl st in first sc. Rep last rnd until bowl is desired height.

Scallop edging

Work same as scallop edging of small bowl—13 scallops.

Large Bowl

Work same as Medium bowl through rnd 10—76 sc.

Rnds 11–16 Ch 1, [sc in each sc to marked sc, 2 sc in marked sc, move marker to last sc made] 4 times; join with sl st in first sc—100 sc at the end of rnd 16.

Bottom ridge (RS) Ch 1, FPsc around each sc; join with sl st in first sc.

Shape sides

Rnd 17 (RS) Ch 1, working into tops of sts of rnd 16, sc in each sc around; join with sl st in first sc.

Note Two decreases (sc2tog) are worked in every other round, to shape sides. Place the decreases randomly within each decrease round. For best results, place the decreases at different locations in each decrease round.

Rnd 18 (decrease) Ch 1, sc in each sc around working two sc2tog to decrease 2 sts anywhere in rnd; join with sl st in first sc—98 sc.

Rnd 19 Ch 1, sc in each sc around; join with sl st in first sc.

Rnds 20–27 Rep last 2 rnds 4 times—90 sc at the end of rnd 27.

Rnd 28 Ch 1, sc in each sc around; join with sl st in first sc. Rep last rnd until bowl is desired height.

Scallop edging

Work same as scallop edging of small bowl—15 scalllops.

Finishing (same for all three bowls)

Weave in ends. Ensure that bottom ridge shows on the outside of bowl. ∎

Shades of Blue Shawl

Shades of Blue Shawl

Large flower motifs are joined as you crochet to create this gorgeously textured wrap, which is then embellished with circular dangles.

Designed by Cristina Mershon

Skill Level: ■■■□

Materials

- 4 3½oz/100g skeins (each approx 462yd/422m) of Noro *Taiyo Sock* (cotton/wool/nylon/silk) in #8 teals/grey/khaki **1**
- Size D/3 (3.25mm) crochet hook OR SIZE TO OBTAIN GAUGE

Size

Instructions are written for one size.

Finished Measurements

29" x 60"/73.5cm x 152.5cm

Gauge

1 motif = 7.25"/18.5cm diameter (picot to picot) using size D/3 (3.25) crochet hook. TAKE TIME TO CHECK GAUGE.

Stitch Glossary

5-dc popcorn Work 5 dc in indicated st. Drop loop from hook. Insert hook from front to back through the top of the first dc of the group. Grab the dropped loop with hook and pull it through the st to close.
4-dc popcorn Work 4 dc in indicated st. Drop loop from hook. Insert hook from front to back through the top of the first dc of the group. Grab the dropped loop with hook and pull it through the st to close.
Shell [3 dc, ch 2, 3 dc] in indicated ch-sp.
Beg shell (beginning shell) [Ch 3, 2 dc, ch 2, 3 dc] in indicated ch-sp.
Picot Ch 3, sc in top of prev dc just made.
Picot shell ([2dc, picot] 4 times) in indicated ch-sp.
Picot join Ch 1, sl st to adjoining motif's picot, ch 1, sc in top of dc just made.
Picot shell join (2 dc, picot, [2 dc, picot join] twice, 2 dc, picot) in indicated ch-sp.

Motif (make 1, join 33)

Note Motifs are joined as work progresses; see assembly diagram (page 141). Do not turn at the end of the rounds, unless noted.
Ch 6 and close with a sl st to form a ring.
Rnd 1 Ch 3 (counts as dc), 23 dc in ring, sl st in top of beg ch—24dc.
Rnd 2 Ch 3, 4-dc popcorn in same sl st, skip 1 dc, ch 2, *5-dc popcorn in next dc, skip 1 dc, ch 2, rep from * around for a total of 12 popcorn sts. Sl st in top of beg ch.
Rnd 3 *Ch 12, skip 5-dc popcorn st, sl st in ch-2 sp, rep from *around for a total of eleven ch-12 sps, ch 6, dtr in sl st that joined rnd 2 (counts as ch-1 sp). (You will finish this rnd on top of the sp.)
Rnd 4 Beg shell in ch-12 sp, ch 2, *shell in next ch-12 sp, ch 2, rep from * around, sl st in top of beg ch—12 shells.
Rnd 5 Sl st in next 2 dc, sl st in ch-2 sp. Beg shell in ch-2 sp, ch 2, sc in next ch-2 sp (between shells), ch 2, *shell in next ch-2 sp (in middle of shell from previous rnd), ch 2, sc in next 2-ch sp, ch 2, rep from * around, sl st in top of beg ch.
Rnd 6 Sl st in next 2 dc, sl st in ch-2 sp. Ch 3, (dc, picot, [2 dc, picot]

3 times) in same ch-2 sp, ch 2, skip ch-2 sp, sc in sc, skip ch-2 sp, ch 2, *picot shell in next ch-2 sp, ch 2, skip ch-2 sp, sc in sc, skip ch-2 sp, ch 2; rep from * around, sl st to top of beg ch, fasten off and weave in ends.

Joining Motifs

Join motifs in vertical columns, following assembly diagram. Each motif labeled "A" joins to 1 other motif; each motif labeled "B" motif joins to 2 other motifs; each motif labeled "C" joins to 3 other motifs.

Join A motifs (join 6)

Rep directions for motif through rnd 5.

Rnd 6 Sl st in next 2 dc, sl st in ch-2 sp. Ch 3, (dc, picot, [2 dc, picot] 3 times) in same ch-2 sp, ch 2, skip ch-2 sp, sc in sc, skip ch-2 sp, ch 2, [picot shell join in next ch-2 sp, ch 2, skip ch-2 sp, sc in sc, skip ch-2 sp, ch 2] twice, *picot shell in next ch-2 sp, ch 2, skip ch-2 sp, sc in sc, skip ch-2 sp, ch 2; rep from * around, sl st to top of beg ch, fasten off and weave in ends.

Join B motifs (join 8)

Rep directions for motif through rnd 5.

Rnd 6 Sl st in next 2 dc, sl st in ch-2 sp. Ch 3, (dc, picot, [2 dc, picot] 3 times) in same ch-2 sp, ch 2, skip ch-2 sp, sc in sc, skip ch-2 sp, ch 2, [picot shell join in next ch-2 sp, ch 2, skip ch-2 sp, sc in sc, skip ch-2 sp, ch 2] 4 times, *picot shell in next ch-2 sp, ch 2, skip ch-2 sp, sc in sc, skip ch-2 sp, ch 2; rep from * around, sl st to top of beg ch, fasten off and weave in ends.

Join C motifs (join 19)

Rep directions for motif through rnd 5.

Rnd 6 Sl st in next 2 dc, sl st in ch-2 sp. Ch 3, (dc, picot, [2 dc, picot] 3 times) in same ch-2 sp, ch 2, skip ch-2 sp, sc in sc, skip ch-2 sp, ch 2, [picot shell in next ch-2 sp, ch 2, skip ch-2 sp, sc in sc, skip ch-2 sp, ch 2] 4 times, *picot shell join in next ch-2 sp, ch 2, skip ch-2 sp, sc in sc, skip ch-2 sp, ch 2; rep from * around to last shell, picot shell in next ch-2 sp, ch 2, skip ch-2 sp, sc in sc, skip ch-2 sp, ch 2, sl st to top of beg ch, fasten off and weave in ends.

Dangling Motif (make 14 pairs)

Note Motifs are joined as work progresses. See assembly diagram for location of motifs.

Ch 6 and close with a sl st to form a ring.

Rnd 1 Ch 3 (counts as dc), 23 dc in ring, sl st in top of beg ch. Ch 12, attach to shawl with sl st, (do not cut the yarn; keep working as follows).

Rnd 2 Ch 12, dc in 4th ch from hook, 10 dc in same ch, sl st in top of beg ch. Fasten off and weave in ends. ∎

(Stitch and assembly diagrams on page 141.)

Engineer Cap

Engineer Cap

No need to hop a freight train to don this jaunty cap. It's playful yet sophisticated, and would look just as stylish worn riding the subway or strolling through the park.

Designed by Ellen Liguori

Skill Level: ■■□□

Materials

- 2 1¾oz/50g skeins (each approx 110yd/100m) of Noro *Kureyon* (wool) in #276 lime/browns/black/navy ③
- Size G/6 (4mm) crochet hook OR SIZE TO OBTAIN GAUGE
- Yarn needle
- 3 ⅝"/1½cm shank buttons

Size
Instructions are written for one size.

Finished Measurements
Circumference 23"/58½cm
Crown diameter 7¼"/18½cm
Height 3¼"/8¼cm

Gauge
17 sts and 20 rows to 4"/10cm over sc using size G/6 (4mm) crochet hook. TAKE TIME TO CHECK GAUGE.

Cap
Crown
Ch 5; join with sl st to first ch to form a ring.
Rnd 1 (RS) Ch 1, 10 sc in ring; join with sl st to first sc—10 sc.
Rnd 2 Ch 1, turn, sc in each st; join with sl st to first sc.
Rnd 3 Ch 1, turn, 2 sc in each st; join with sl st to first sc—20 sc.
Rnd 4 Ch 1, turn, sc in each st; join with sl st to first sc.
Rnd 5 Ch 2 (counts as first dc here and throughout), turn, 2 dc in each st; join with sl st to top of beginning ch—40 dc.
Rnds 6–8 Ch 1, turn, sc in each st; join with sl st to first sc.
Rnd 9 Rep rnd 5—80 dc.
Rnds 10–12 Rep rnd 6.
Rnd 13 Ch 1, turn, sc in first 2 st, * 2 sc in next st, sc in next 2 st; rep from *; join with sl st to first sc, do not fasten off—106 sc.
Block crown to 7 ¼"/18.5cm diameter.
Rim
Note Work on RS only, do not turn.
Rnd 14 Working tbl, ch 1, sc in each st; join with sl st to first sc.
Rnds 15–21 Ch 1, sc in each st; join with sl st to first sc.
Rnd 22 Working tbl, ch 1, sc in each st; join with sl st to first sc.
Rnd 23 Ch 2, dc in each st; join with sl st to top of beginning ch.
Rnd 24 Rep rnd 22.
Rnd 25 Rep rnd 15.
Fasten off leaving a long tail. Thread tail through yarn needle and embroider a satin st up the side along the joining st of each round.
Brim
Note Continue working in rows.
With RS facing place a marker 6 sts to the left of faux seam. Join yarn with sl st to first st left of marker.
Row 1 Working tfl, ch 1, sc in first 2 st, hdc in next st, dc in next 27 st, hdc in next st, sc in next 2 st, leave rem st unworked—33 sts.
Row 2 Working tfl, ch 1, turn, skip first sc, sc in next 2 st, hdc in next

st, dc in next 25 st, hdc in next st, sc in next 2 st, leave rem st unworked—31 sts.

Row 3 Ch 1, turn, skip first sc, sc in next 2 st, hdc across to last 3 st, sc in next 2 st, leave rem st unworked—29 sts.

Row 4 Working tfl, rep brim row 3, fasten off—27 sts.

Row 5 With RS facing, join yarn with sl st to right side of brim, sc loosely in each st around the brim.

Edging rnd Ch 1, turn, sl st tfl in each st around cap; join with sl st to first ch, fasten off.

Weave in ends. Sew buttons to front side of cap between the faux seam and brim.

To tighten the cap, work rnd 13 as follows to the desired size:

Rnd 13 Ch 1, turn, *sc in next 3 (4) st, 2 sc in next sc; rep from *; join with sl st to first sc—100 (96) sts.

To loosen the cap, work rnd 13 as follows:

Rnd 13 Ch 1, turn, *sc in next st, 2 sc in next st; rep from *; join with sl st to first sc—120 sts.

All other rows remain the same. ∎

Granny Square Purse

Granny Square Purse

Grannies aren't just for afghans anymore! Joining them into a sophisticated purse takes them to a new level of style.

Designed by Candi Jensen

Skill Level: ■■□□

Materials

- 3 1¾oz/50g skeins (each approx 110yd/100m) of Noro *Kureyon* (wool) in #256 pink/orange/teal (A) (4)
- 1 skein 1.76oz/50g skeins (each approx 110yd/100m) of Noro *Kureyon* (wool) in #276 lime/browns/black/navy (B)
- Size H/8 (5mm) crochet hook OR SIZE TO OBTAIN GAUGE
- Round braided leather purse handle, 24"/61cm long, in dark brown
- Sharp sewing needle and strong thread (for sewing handle to purse)
- 1yd/1m fabric (for optional lining)
- Fabric marker (for marking optional lining fabric)
- Sewing needle and thread or sewing machine (for optional lining)
- Yarn needle

Size

Instructions are written for one size.

Finished Measurements

Approx 14"/35.5cm wide (at widest) x 14"/35.5cm tall (at tallest)

Note

Purse is made from 13 granny squares. The granny squares are arranged as shown in assembly diagram and sewn together. Top edging is then added and the purse handle sewn in place.

Gauge

One granny square measures 5 x 5"/12.5 x 12.5cm using H/8 (5mm) crochet hook. TAKE TIME TO CHECK GAUGE.

Stitch Glossary

sc2tog (single crochet 2 stitches together) [Insert hook in next stitch and draw up a loop] twice, yarn over and draw through all 3 loops on hook.

Granny Square (make 13)

With A, make an adjustable ring.
Rnd 1 (RS) Ch 2 (counts as first hdc), 2 hdc in ring, [ch 1, 3 hdc in ring] 3 times, ch 1; join with sl st in top of beg ch—four 3-hdc groups, and 4 corner ch-1 sps.
Rnd 2 (WS) Ch 3 (counts as first dc here and throughout), turn, (2 dc, ch 1, 3 dc) in first ch-1 sp, dc in center hdc of next 3-hdc group, *(3 dc, ch 1, 3 dc) in next ch-1 sp, dc in center hdc of next 3-hdc group; rep from * around; join with sl st in top of beg ch—28 dc (7 dc across each side), and 4 corner ch-1 sps. Fasten off A.
Rnd 3 With RS facing, draw up a loop of B in any corner ch-1 sp, ch 3, (2 dc, ch 1, 3 dc) in same ch-1 sp, sk next dc, dc in next 5 dc (the 5 center dc of 7-dc side), *(3 dc, ch 1, 3 dc) in next ch-1 sp, sk next dc, dc in next 5 dc; rep from * around; join with sl st in top of beg ch—44 dc (11 dc across each side), and 4 corner ch-1 sps. Fasten off B.
Rnd 4 With WS facing, draw up a loop of A in any corner ch-1 sp, ch 3, (2 dc, ch 1, 3 dc) in same ch-1 sp, sk next dc, dc in next 9 dc, *(3 dc, ch 1, 3 dc) in next ch-1 sp, sk next dc, dc in next 9 dc; rep from * around; join with sl st in top of beg ch—60 dc (15 across each side), and 4 corner ch-1 sps. Fasten off A.

Finishing

Arrange granny squares as shown in assembly diagram and sew together.
Lining (optional)
Fold fabric in half. Flatten purse and place on top of fabric. With

fabric marker, trace around edge of purse. Remove purse and cut along the trace line, cutting two lining pieces. With RS of lining pieces together, sew side and lower edges together, leaving about a ½"/1.5cm seam allowance. Fold about ½"/1.5cm of top edges to WS and press. Turn crocheted purse inside out. Place liner over purse, with RS of fabric facing out. Sew top edges of liner to top edges of purse, just below top edge of purse. Sew lower corners of liner to lower corners of purse with a few stitches, to anchor. Turn purse right side out, pushing liner to the inside of the purse.

Note Take care to ensure that the sewing stitches do not show on outside of purse.

Top edging

With RS facing, join A with sc in join between granny squares at one top point of purse; working around top edge, sc in next 14 dc, sc2tog (working first leg in last sc of current granny square and 2nd leg in first sc of next granny square), sc in next 14 dc, sc in join between granny squares (at opposite top point), sc in next 14 dc, sc2tog (working first leg in last sc of current granny square and 2nd leg in first sc of next granny square), sc in next 14 dc; join with sl st in first sc.

Weave in ends. Sew ends of handle to top points. ∎

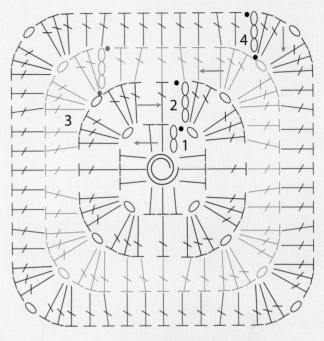

Granny Square

Stitch Key

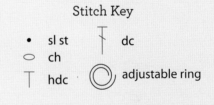

- • sl st
- ○ ch
- T hdc
- T dc
- ◎ adjustable ring

Leave these edges unsewn for top opening. Sew all other edges together.

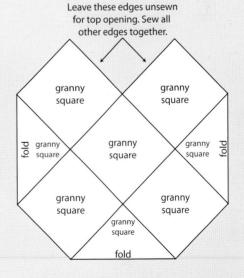

granny square · granny square · fold · granny square · granny square · granny square · granny square · fold · granny square · granny square · fold

Assembly Diagram (Front and Back)

Granny Triangle Cowl

Granny Triangle Cowl

Squares aren't the only shapes to get the classic granny treatment. Whip up a fun neck warmer by joining together six granny triangles.

Designed by Angela Tong

Skill Level: ■■□□

Materials
- 2 1¾oz/50g skeins (each approx 110yd/100m) of Noro *Kureyon* (wool) in #250 purple/red/royal (**4**)
- Size H/8 (5mm) crochet hook OR SIZE TO OBTAIN GAUGE
- Yarn needle

Size
Instructions are written for one size.

Finished Measurements
Circumference approx 8"/20.5cm wide x 26"/66cm

Notes
1) Cowl is made from 6 granny triangles. Triangles are arranged as shown in assembly diagram, and side edges slip-stitched together to form a ring.
2) Each granny triangle is worked in joined rounds with RS facing at all times.

Gauge
One granny triangle measures 6¼"/16.5cm across side edge, using H/8 (5mm) crochet hook. TAKE TIME TO CHECK GAUGE.

Granny Triangle (make 6)
Ch 4; join with sl st in first ch to form a ring.

Rnd 1 (RS) Ch 6 (counts as dc, ch 3 here and throughout), [3 dc in ring, ch 3] twice, 2 dc in ring; join with sl st in 3rd ch of beg ch—three 3-dc groups, and 3 ch-3 sps.

Rnd 2 Sl st in each st to center of first ch-3 sp, ch 6, 3 dc in same ch-3 sp, *ch 1, (3 dc, ch 3, 3 dc) in next ch-3 sp (corner made); rep from * once more, ch 1, 2 dc in same ch-3 sp as beg; join with sl st in 3rd ch of beg ch—three (3 dc, ch 3, 3 dc) corners, and 3 ch-1 sps.

Rnd 3 Sl st in each st to center of first ch-3 sp, ch 6, 3 dc in same ch-3 sp, *ch 1, 3 dc in next ch-1 sp, ch 1, (3 dc, ch 3, 3 dc) in next corner ch-3 sp; rep from * once more, ch 1, 3 dc in next ch-1 sp, ch 1, 2 dc in same ch-3 sp as beg; join with sl st in 3rd ch of beg ch—three corners, and one 3-dc group across each side.

Rnd 4 Sl st in each st to center of first ch-3 sp, ch 6, 3 dc in same ch-3 sp, *[ch 1, 3 dc in next ch-1 sp] twice, ch 1, (3 dc, ch 3, 3 dc) in next corner ch-3 sp; rep from * once more, [ch 1, 3 dc in next ch-1 sp] twice, ch 1, 2 dc in same ch-3 sp as beg; join with sl st in 3rd ch of beg ch—three corners, and two 3-dc group across each side.

Rnd 5 Sl st in each st to center of first ch-3 sp, ch 6, 3 dc in same ch-3 sp, *[ch 1, 3 dc in next ch-1 sp] 3 times, ch 1, (3 dc, ch 3, 3 dc) in next corner ch-3 sp; rep from * once more, [ch 1, 3 dc in next ch-1 sp] 3 times, ch 1, 2 dc in same ch-3 sp as beg; join with sl st in 3rd ch of beg ch—three corners, and three 3-dc group across each side. Fasten off.

Finishing
Arrange triangles as shown in assembly diagram. Join side edges of neighboring triangles, as follows: Hold neighboring triangles with RS together. From WS, working through both thicknesses and in both loops of each st on both triangles, join yarn with sl st at beg of edge, sl st across edge. Fasten off. Rep until all 6 triangles are joined in a strip, then join the edges of the first and last triangles to form a ring.

Edging
With RS facing, draw up a loop anywhere in one edge of cowl.

Rnd 1 Ch 3 (counts as dc), dc evenly spaced around edge of cowl; join with sl st in top of beg ch.

Rnd 2 Ch 1, rev sc in each dc around; join with sl st in beg ch. Fasten off. Rep around other edge of cowl.

Weave in ends. Wet block to finished measurements. ■

Stitch Key

- • sl st
- ◯ ch
- ┼ dc

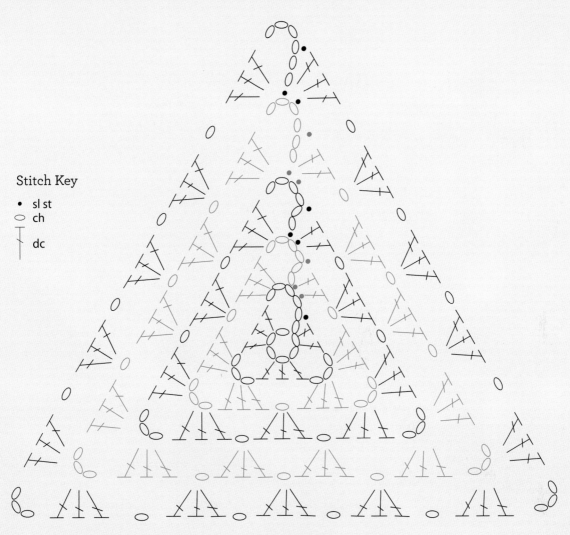

Granny Triangle

2. Join edges of first and last triangle to form a ring.

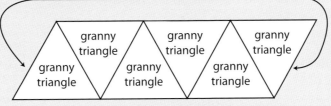

1. Join edges of neighboring triangles to form a strip.

Assembly Diagram

Cap-Sleeve Cardigan

Cap-Sleeve Cardigan

This sweetly feminine cardi features a simple double crochet pattern with pretty shell-stitch edgings. Wear it with a dress or to pretty up jeans.

Designed by Yoko Hatta

Skill Level: ■■☐☐

Materials

- 3 (3, 4) 3½oz/100g skeins (each approx 462yd/422m) of Noro *Taiyo Sock* (cotton/wool/nylon/silk) in #1 black/charcoal/purple/blue ❶
- Size B/1 (2.25mm) crochet hook OR SIZE TO OBTAIN GAUGE
- ¹¹⁄₁₆"/18mm diameter button

Sizes

Instructions are written for sizes Small (Medium, Large); shown in size Small.

Finished Measurements

Bust 36 (40, 44)"91½ (101.5, 111.5)cm

Gauge

26 dc and 12 rows = 4"/10cm using size B/1 (2.25mm) crochet hook. TAKE TIME TO CHECK GAUGE.

Stitch Glossary

dc2tog (double crochet 2 together) (Yo and insert hook in st, yo and draw up a loop, yo and draw through first two loops on hook) twice, yo and draw through rem 3 loops on hook.
Shell Work 5 dc in same st.

Cardigan

Ch 235 (263, 289).
Row 1 (RS) Dc in 3rd ch from hook (counts as first dc) and each ch across—233 (261, 287) dc. Turn.
Row 2 Ch 3 (counts as first dc, here and throughout), dc in each dc across. Turn. **Row 3** Rep row 1.
Row 4 Ch 4 (count as first dc + ch 1), *skip next dc, dc in next dc, ch 1; rep from * across, end dc in last dc. Turn.
Row 5 Ch 3, dc in each ch-1 sp and dc across to beg ch, dc in 4th and 3rd ch of beg ch. Turn.
Rep rows 2–5 until piece measures 10¾ (12, 13¼)", ending with row 4.

Back panel

Skip 70 (77, 85) sts. Join yarn to sl st to next st.
Row 1 Ch 3, dc in ea ch-1 sp and dc across for a total of 92 (106, 116) dc, leave remaining sts unworked. Turn—93 (107, 117) dc.
Rows 2–3 Ch 3, dc in ea dc across. Fasten off. Turn.
Row 4 Skip 47 (53, 59) sts from edge of front collar edge, join yarn with sl st in next st. Ch 77 (83, 89), dc in first dc of back panel (skip sts count as underarm), *ch 1, skip next dc, dc in next dc; rep from * across back panel, ch 77 (83, 89), skip 22 (23, 25) sts (skip sts count as underarm), sl st to next st. Fasten off. Turn.

Yoke

Row 1 (RS) Join yarn to beg of row with sl st, ch 3, dc in ea ch-1 sp, dc, and ch across. Turn—341 (379, 413) dc.
Rows 2–3 Ch 3, dc in ea dc across. Turn.
Row 4 Ch 4, skip first 2 dc, dc in next dc, *ch 1, skip next dc, dc in next dc; rep from * across. Turn.
Row 5 (dec row) Ch 3, dc in next 4 sts, *dc2tog over next 2 sts, dc in next 7 sts; rep from * across to last 3 (5, 3) sts, dc in each st across. Turn—304 (338, 368) dc.
Rows 6–7 Rep rows 2–3
Row 8 Ch 3, skip first dc, dc in next dc, *ch 1, skip next dc, dc in next dc; rep from * across. Turn.
Row 9 (dec row) Ch 3, dc in next 4 sts, *dc2tog over next 2 sts, dc in next 6 sts; rep from * across to last 3 (5, 3) sts, dc in each st across. Turn—267 (297, 323) dc. **Rows 10–12** Rep rows 2–4.
Row 13 (dec row) Ch 3, dc in next 4 sts, *dc2tog over next 2 sts, dc in next 5 sts; rep from * across to last 3 (5, 3) sts, dc in each st across. Turn—230 (256, 278) dc.

Rows 14–15 Rep rows 2–3. **Row 16** Rep row 8.

Row 17 (dec row) Ch 3, dc in next 4 sts, *dc2tog over next 2 sts, dc in next 4 sts; rep from * across to last 3 (5, 3) sts, dc in each st across. Turn—193 (215, 233) dc. **Rows 18–20** Rep rows 2–4.

Row 21 (dec row) Ch 3, dc in next 4 sts, *dc2tog over next 2 sts, dc in next 3 sts; rep from * across to last 3 (5, 3) sts, dc in each st across. Turn—156 (174, 188) dc. **Row 22** Rep row 2.

Size Small only Fasten off.

Sizes Medium and Large

Rows 23–24 Rep rows 3 and 8.

Row 25 (dec row) Ch 3, dc in next 8 (4) sts, *dc2tog over next 2 sts, dc in next (7) sts; rep from * across to last 3 sts, dc in each st to end. Turn—(156, 168) dc. **Row 26** Rep row 2.

Size Medium only Fasten off.

Size Large

Rows 27–28 Rep rows 3 and 8.

Row 29 (dec row) Ch 3, dc in next 8 sts, *dc2tog over next 2 sts, dc in next 11 sts; rep from * across to last 3 sts, dc in each st to end. Turn—156 dc. **Row 30** Rep row 2. Fasten off.

Finishing

Cuff edging
Rnd 1 Ch 1, sc evenly around, ending with a multiple of 6 sts, join with sl st to first sc.

Rnd 2 Ch 1, *sc in next sc, skip next 2 sc, shell in next sc, skip next 2 sc; rep from * around, join with sl st to first sc. Fasten off.

Collar edging
Mark location of buttonhole on right front. Work cuff edging pattern around lower edge, center fronts, and neck. On rnd 1, at buttonhole marker work ch 5, skip 2 row ends and cont in cuff edging directions. Weave in ends. Block. Sew button opposite buttonhole. ■

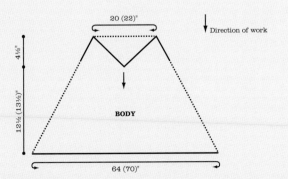

Chevron Hat

Chevron Hat

Alternating rounds of two colors of *Silk Garden Sock* zigzag up and down and all around this lovely cap. Diamond shapes stitched in *Baby Cashmerino* from Debbie Bliss add pretty accents.

Designed by Lily Chin

Skill Level: ■■■□

Materials
- 1 3½oz/100g skein (each approx 328yd/300m) of Noro *Silk Garden Sock* (wool/silk/nylon/mohair) in #252 black/lime/blue (A) and #268 green/aqua/brown (B) **2**
- 1 1¾oz/50g skein (each approx 137yd/125m) of Debbie Bliss *Baby Cashmerino* (merino wool/microfiber/cashmere) in #340059 mallard **2**
- Size G/7 (4.5mm) crochet hook OR SIZE TO OBTAIN GAUGE
- Yarn needle

Size
Instructions are written for one size.

Finished Measurements
Circumference approx 7"/18cm deep x 21"/53.5cm

Notes
1) Hat is worked, beginning at top, in a chevron pattern changing color every round.
2) After the top of the hat is complete, diamonds are worked into the "valleys" of the chevrons. Each diamond is worked back and forth in rows.
3) After the diamonds are inserted, work resumes in the chevron pattern worked in rounds.
4) To change color, work last stitch of old color to last yarn over. Yarn over with new color and draw through all loops on hook to complete stitch. Proceed with new color. Do not fasten off old color unless otherwise instructed. Carry color not in use up inside of piece until next needed.

Gauge
16 sts and 18 rows = 4"/10cm over single crochet using G/7 (4.5mm) crochet hook. TAKE TIME TO CHECK GAUGE.

Stitch Glossary
double-dec (double decrease) Draw up loop in next stitch, skip next stitch, draw up loop in next stitch, yarn over and draw through all 3 loops on hook—2 sts decreased.

Hat
Rnd 1 (WS) With A, *ch 7 loosely, working in back lps only, sc in 3rd ch from hook (skipped 2 ch counts as ch-2 sp at tip of petal) and in next 4 ch across (one petal made); rep from * 5 more times for 6 petals; taking care not to twist, join with sl st in first ch (beside beg sl knot)—6 petals (each consisting of 5 sc). Fasten off, leaving an 8"/20.5cm tail.
Rnd 2 (RS) With RS facing, draw up a lp of B in ch-2 sp at tip of any petal, ch 1, *sc in bottom of next 4 ch, draw up a lp in bottom of next ch, draw up a lp in next sc (of next petal), yo and draw through all 3 lps on hook (sc2tog made), sc in next 4 sc, sc in next ch-2 sp at tip of petal; rep from * around working last sc in same ch-2 sp as beg, change to A and join with sl st in first sc—60 sts. Do not fasten off B.
Rnd 3 With A, ch 1, turn, sc in first sc, *sc in next 3 sc, double-dec, sc in next 3 sc**, 3 sc in next sc (2 sts increased); rep from * around ending last rep at **, 2 sc in same sc as beg, change to B and join

with sl st in first sc. Do not fasten off A.

Rnd 4 With B, rep rnd 3, change to A and join with sl st in first sc.

Rnd 5 Rep rnd 3.

Rnd 6 With B, ch 1, turn, sc in first sc, *sc in next 9 sc**, 3 sc in next sc; rep from * around ending last rep at **, 2 sc in same sc as beg, change to A and join with sl st in first sc—72 sts.

Rnd 7 With A, ch 1, turn, sc in first sc, *sc in next 4 sc, double-dec, sc in next 4 sc**, 3 sc in next sc; rep from * around ending last rep at **, 2 sc in same sc as beg, change to B and join with sl st in first sc.

Rnd 8 With B, ch 1, turn, sc in first sc, *sc in next 11 sc**, 3 sc in next sc; rep from * around ending last rep at **, 2 sc in same sc as beg, change to A and join with sl st in first sc—84 sts.

Rnd 9 With A, ch 1, turn, sc in first sc, *sc in next 5 sc, double-dec, sc in next 5 sc**, 3 sc in next sc; rep from * around ending last rep at **, 2 sc in same sc as beg, change to B and join with sl st in first sc.

Rnd 10 With B, ch 1, turn, sc in first sc, *sc in next 13 sc**, 3 sc in next sc; rep from * around ending last rep at **, 2 sc in same sc as beg, change to A and join with sl st in first sc—96 sts.

Rnd 11 With A, ch 1, turn, sc in first sc, *sc in next 6 sc, double-dec, sc in next 6 sc**, 3 sc in next sc; rep from * around ending last rep at **, 2 sc in same sc as beg, change to B and join with sl st in first sc.

Rnd 12 With B, ch 1, turn, sc in first sc, *sc in next 15 sc**, 3 sc in next sc; rep from * around ending last rep at **, 2 sc in same sc as beg, change to A and join with sl st in first sc—108 sts.

Rnd 13 (WS) With A, ch 1, turn, sc in first sc, *sc in next 7 sc, double-dec, sc in next 7 sc**, 3 sc in next sc; rep from * around ending last rep at **, 2 sc in same sc as beg, change to B and join with sl st in first sc. Do not fasten off A. Drop loop of B from hook. You may wish to put the dropped loop on a stitch marker or safety pin to ensure that it does not unravel.

Diamonds

Row 1 (RS) With RS facing, join C with sc in 4th sc following any 3-sc group, sc in next 2 sc, double-dec (centered over "valley"), sc in next 3 sc—7 sts.

Row 2 Ch 1, turn, sc in first 2 sc, double-dec, sc in last 2 sc—5 sts.

Row 3 Ch 1, turn, sc in first sc, double-dec, sc in last sc—3 sts.

Row 4 Ch 1, turn, double-dec—1 st. Fasten off.

Rep to work a diamond in every "valley" of the chevron pattern.

Continue chevron pattern

Return dropped lp of B to hook.

Rnd 14 (RS) With RS facing and B, ch 1, sc in first sc, *sc in next 4 sc, sc in end of next 3 rows of diamond, 3 sc in corner of diamond, sc in end of next 3 rows of diamond, sc in next 4 sc**, 3 sc in next sc; rep from * around ending last rep at **, 2 sc in same sc as beg,

change to A and join with sl st in first sc—120 sts. Do not fasten off B.

Rnd 15 With A, ch 1, turn, sc in first sc, *sc in next 3 sc, double-dec, sc in next 3 sc**, 3 sc in next sc; rep from * around ending last rep at **, 2 sc in same sc as beg, change to B and join with sl st in first sc. Do not fasten off A.

Rnd 16 With B, rep rnd 15, change to A and join with sl st in first sc. Do not fasten off B.

Rnds 17–20 Rep rnds 15 and 16 twice.

Rnd 21 (WS) With A, turn, *sl st in next sc, sc in next sc, hdc in next sc, dc in next sc, yo twice, draw up a lp in next sc, [yo and draw through 2 lps on hook] twice, sk next sc, yo twice, draw up a lp in next sc, [yo and draw through 2 lps on hook] twice, yo and draw through all 3 loops on hook, dc in next sc, hdc in next sc, sc in next sc; rep from * around, change to B and join with sl st in first sl st—96 sts.

Rnd 22 With B, ch 1, turn, sc in each st around, skipping all sl sts, change to A and join with sl st in first sc—84 sts. Fasten off B.

Rnd 23 With A, ch 1, turn, sc in each sc around; join with sl st in first sc. Fasten off.

Finishing

Thread long beg tail through stitches around hole at top of hat and pull to gather and close opening. Secure end. Weave in ends. ∎

Ruffled Scarf

Ruffled Scarf

A double layer of ruffles at each end of this airy scarf puts a more feminine spin on the geometric mesh design.

Designed by Valentina Devine

Skill Level: ■■☐☐

Materials

- 5 1¾oz/50g skeins (each approx 110yd/100m) of Noro *Silk Garden* (silk/mohair/lambswool) in #337 blues/greens/pinks **③**
- Size E/4 (3.5mm) crochet hook OR SIZE TO OBTAIN GAUGE

Size

Instructions are written for one size.

Finished Measurements

10"/25.5cm wide x 70"/177.5cm long

Gauge

20 sts and 5 rows to 4"/10cm over pattern stitch using E/4 (3.5mm) crochet hook. TAKE TIME TO CHECK GAUGE.

Scarf

Ch 53.

Row 1 Tr in 5th ch from hook (counts as first tr, here and throughout), tr, *ch 2, sk 2 ch, tr in next 2 ch; rep from * across—13 tr groups.

Row 2 Ch 4, tr, *ch 2, tr in next 2 tr; rep from * across—13 tr groups. Rep row 2 until piece measures 70"/177.5cm. Do not fasten off.

Ruffle

Row 1 Ch 1, work sc between each cluster of 2 tr and 2 sc in each ch-2 sp across—37 sc.

Row 2 Ch 4, 2 tr in first sc, 3 tr in each sc across—37 sets of 3-tr.

Row 3 (picot) Ch 1, *sc in each sc to center of 3-tr group, ch 3, sl st in 3rd ch from hook; rep from * across. Fasten off.

Attach yarn at base of next row of mesh. Repeat ruffle.

Rep both ruffles on opposite end of scarf. ■

Shell Stitch Tunic

Shell Stitch Tunic

Crocheted in bubblegum pink, juicy orange, apple green, and other irresistible shades (all one colorway), this light, sleeveless tunic is the epitome of fun summer fashion.

Designed by Wei Wilkins

Skill Level: ■■■□

Materials
- 3 (4, 4) 3½oz/100g skeins (each approx 462yd/422m) of Noro *Taiyo Sock* (cotton/wool/nylon/silk) in #7 rose/yellow/pistachio (**1**)
- Size 3 (2.1mm) steel crochet hook OR SIZE TO OBTAIN GAUGE
- Stitch markers
- Yarn needle

Sizes
Instructions are written for size Small (Medium/Large, X-Large); shown in size Small.

Finished Measurements
Bust 34 (39, 43)"/86.5 (99, 109)cm
Length (from back neck) 26½ (27, 27½)"/67 (68.5, 70)cm

Notes
1) Tunic is made from two pieces: front and back. Both pieces are worked in two stages. The bodice is worked from the waist up to the shoulders. Then the skirt is worked from the waist down to the lower edge.
2) Shoulders and sides are seamed, then edging is worked around lower, armhole, and neck edges.

Gauge
7 shells and 14 rows to 5"/12.5cm over shell pattern using size 3 (2.1mm) steel crochet hook. TAKE TIME TO CHECK GAUGE.

Stitch Glossary
2-dc Cl (2 double crochet cluster) Yo, insert hook in indicated st or space and draw up a loop, yo and draw through 2 loops on hook (2 loops remain on hook); yo, insert hook in *same* st or space and draw up a loop, yo and draw through 2 loops on hook, yo and draw through all 3 loops on hook.
dc-tr2tog (double crochet-treble crochet 2 sts together) Yo, insert hook in indicated st or space (for first leg) and draw up a loop, yo and draw through 2 loops on hook (2 loops remain on hook); [yo] twice, insert hook in next indicated st or space (for 2nd leg) and draw up a loop (5 loops on hook), [yo and draw through 2 loops on hook] twice, yo and draw through all 3 loops on hook.
shell (2 dc, ch 2, 2 dc) in indicated stitch or space.

Back Bodice
Ch 124 (139, 154).
Row 1 (RS) Shell in 6th ch from hook, *sk next 4 ch, shell in next ch; rep from * across to last 3 ch, sk next 2 ch, dc in last ch—24 (27, 30) shells.
Rows 2–17 Ch 3 (counts as dc here and throughout), turn, shell in ch-2 sp of each shell across, dc in top of beg ch.
Shape armholes
Row 1 Turn, [ch 4, sl st in ch-2 sp of next shell] 1 (2, 3) time(s), ch 3, dc in same ch-2 sp, shell in ch-2 sp of each shell across to last 1 (2, 3) shell(s), ch 3, sl st in ch-2 sp of next shell, tr in next ch-sp (this ch-sp

will be the top of the beg ch for the smallest size and the ch-2 sp of the next shell for the larger sizes)—22 (23, 24) shells.

Row 2 Ch 3, turn, shell in ch-2 sp of first shell, shell in ch-2 sp of each shell across to last shell, dc in ch-2 sp of last shell, work dc-tr2tog working first leg in same ch-2 sp and 2nd leg in top of beg ch—21 (22, 23) shells.

Rows 3–5 Rep last row 3 times—18 (19, 20) shells.

Row 6 Ch 3, turn, shell in ch-2 sp of each shell across, dc in top of beg ch. Rep last row until armhole measures 8 (8½, 9)"/20.5 (21.5, 23)cm.

Shape first shoulder

Row 1 Ch 5, turn, sc in ch-2 sp of first shell, ch 2, (2 hdc, ch 2, 2 hdc) in ch-2 sp of next 1 (1, 2) shell(s), shell in ch-2 sp of next shell, (2 dc, ch 2, dc) in ch-2 sp of next shell, dc-tr2tog working first leg in same ch-2 sp and 2nd leg in next sp between shells; leave rem sts un-worked (for back neck and 2nd shoulder).

Row 2 Ch 4, turn, sl st in first ch-2 sp, [ch 4, sl st in next ch-2 sp] 2 (2, 3) times, ch 4, sl st in next sc; leave rem ch-sp unworked. Fasten off.

Shape second shoulder

Row 1 Join yarn with sl st in same sp between shells of 2nd leg of dc-tr2tog at end of row 1 of first shoulder, ch 3, sl st in ch-2 sp of next shell, *ch 4, sl st in ch-2 sp of next shell; rep from * across to last 4 (4, 5) shells, ch 3, sl st in next sp between shells (between 5th [5th, 6th] and 4th [4th, 5th] to last shell), ch 3, shell in ch-2 sp of next 2 shells, (2 hdc, ch 2, 2 hdc) in ch-2 sp of next 1 (1, 2) shell(s), ch 2, sc in ch-2 sp of last shell, tr in top of beg ch.

Row 2 Ch 4, turn, sl st in first sc, [ch 4, sl st in next ch-2 sp] 3 (3, 4) times, ch 1, dc in top of next ch 3. Fasten off.

Back Skirt

Row 1 (RS) With RS facing, working across opposite side of founda-tion ch, draw up a loop in first ch, ch 3, sk next 2 ch, shell in next ch (at base of shell in row 1 of bodice), *sk next 4 ch, shell in next ch; rep from * across working a shell in the ch at base of each shell in row 1 of bodice, sk next 2 ch, dc in next ch (at base of beg ch of bodice).

Note Skirt shaping is achieved by working chains between the shells. The additional chains are added gradually.

Place 8 (9, 10) stitch markers in the spaces between shells, evenly spaced across the row. Move markers up into the ch-spaces as row is worked.

Rows 3–6 Ch 3, turn, *shell in ch-2 sp of each shell to next marker, ch 1; rep from * until all markers have been reached, shell in ch-2 sp of each rem shell across, dc in top of beg ch.

Place 8 (9, 10) more markers in unmarked spaces between shells, evenly spaced across row.

Rows 7–12 Rep row 3.
Remove markers.

Rows 13–18 Ch 3, turn, *shell in ch-2 sp of next shell, ch 1; rep from * across to last shell, shell in ch-2 sp of last shell, dc in top of beg ch. Place a marker in space between first and 2nd shell, then in every other space between shells (leave last space of medium size un-marked)

Rows 19–25 Ch 3, turn, shell in ch-2 sp of each shell across, working ch 1 at each unmarked space between shells and ch 2 at each marked space between shells.
Remove markers.

Rows 26–34 Ch 3, turn, *shell in ch-2 sp of next shell, ch 2; rep from * across to last shell, shell in ch-2 sp of last shell, dc in top of beg ch. Fasten off.

Front

Work same as back until armholes measure 2½"/6.5cm (ensure that armhole shaping is complete).

Shape first shoulder

Row 1 Ch 3, turn, shell in ch-2 sp of first 5 (5, 6) shells, 2-dc Cl in ch-2 sp of next shell; leave rem sts unworked (for front neck and 2nd shoulder)—5 (5, 6) shells.

Row 2 Ch 3, turn, shell in ch-2 sp of each shell across, dc in top of beg ch.

Row 3 Ch 3, turn, shell in ch-2 sp of first 4 (4, 5) shells, dc in ch-2 sp of next shell, work dc-tr2tog working first leg in same ch-2 sp and 2nd leg in top of beg ch—4 (4, 5) shells.

Row 4 Ch 3, turn, dc in next dc, shell in ch-2 sp of each shell across, dc in top of beg ch.

Rows 5–15 (17, 19) Ch 3, turn, shell in ch-2 sp of each shell across, dc in top of beg ch.

Row 16 (18, 20) Ch 3, turn, shell in ch-2 sp of first 2 shells, (2 hdc, ch 2, 2 hdc) in ch-2 sp of next 1 (1, 2) shell(s), ch 2, sc in ch-2 sp of last shell, tr in top of beg ch.

Row 17 (19, 21) [Ch 4, sl st in next ch-2 sp] 3 (3, 4) times, ch 1, dc in top of next ch 3. Fasten off.

Shape second shoulder

Row 1 Join yarn with sl st in same ch-2 sp as 2-dc Cl at end of row 1 of first shoulder, *ch 4, sl st in ch-2 sp of next shell; rep from * across to last 6 (6, 7) shells, ch 4, (sl st, ch 2, dc) in ch-2 sp of next shell, shell in ch-2 sp of next 5 (5, 6) shells, dc in top of beg ch—5 (5, 6) shells.

Row 2 Ch 3, turn, shell in ch-2 sp of next 5 (5, 6) shells, dc in top of next ch-3.

Row 3 Ch 3, turn, 2 dc in ch-2 sp of first shell, shell in ch-2 sp of next 4 (4, 5) shells, dc in top of beg ch—4 (4, 5) shells.

Row 4 Ch 3, turn, shell in ch-2 sp of each shell across, 2 dc in top of beg ch.

Rows 5–15 (17, 19) Ch 3, turn, shell in ch-2 sp of each shell across, dc in top of beg ch.

Row 16 (18, 20) Ch 4, turn, sc in ch-2 sp of first shell, ch 2, (2 hdc, ch 2, 2 hdc) in ch-2 sp of each of next 1 (1, 2) shell(s), shell in ch-2 sp of next shell, (2 dc, ch 2, dc) in ch-2 sp of next shell, dc-tr2tog working first leg in same ch-2 sp and 2nd leg in top of beg ch.

Row 17 (19, 21) Ch 4, turn, sl st in first ch-2 sp, [ch 4, sl st in next ch-2 sp] 2 (2, 3) times, ch 4, sl st in next sc; leave rem ch-sp unworked. Fasten off.

Front Skirt

Work same as back skirt.

Drawstring

Ch 400.

Row 1 Sc in 2nd ch from hook and in each ch across. Fasten off.

Finishing

Hold RS of front and back together with shoulder stitches matching, sl st across to seam shoulders. With RS of front and back together, sl st side seams together.

Lower edging

With RS facing, draw up a loop in ch-2 sp of any shell, ch 7, sl st in 3rd ch from hook, (dc, [ch 4, sl st in 3rd ch from hook, dc] 3 times) in same ch-2 sp, (dc, [ch 4, sl st in 3rd ch from hook, dc] 4 times) in ch-2 sp of each shell around (sk the ch-2 sps between shells); join with sl st in 3rd ch of beg ch. Fasten off.

Armhole edging

With RS facing, draw up a loop at underarm, work picot edging as follows: Ch 1, *work 4 sc evenly spaced across edge, ch 3, sl st in 3rd ch from hook (picot made); rep from * around; join with sl st in first sc. Fasten off. Rep around other armhole.

Neck edging

With RS facing, draw up a loop in one shoulder seam, work picot edging around neck edge, same as armhole picot edging. Fasten off. Block lightly, if desired. Weave in ends. Beg at center front, weave drawstring through shells of row 2 of bodice, alternately weaving under 2 shells and over 1 shell. ∎

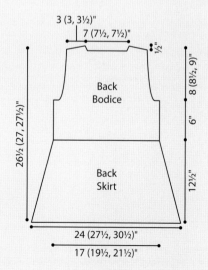

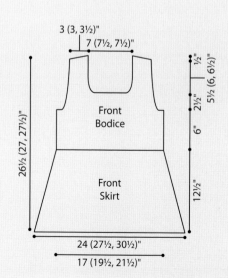

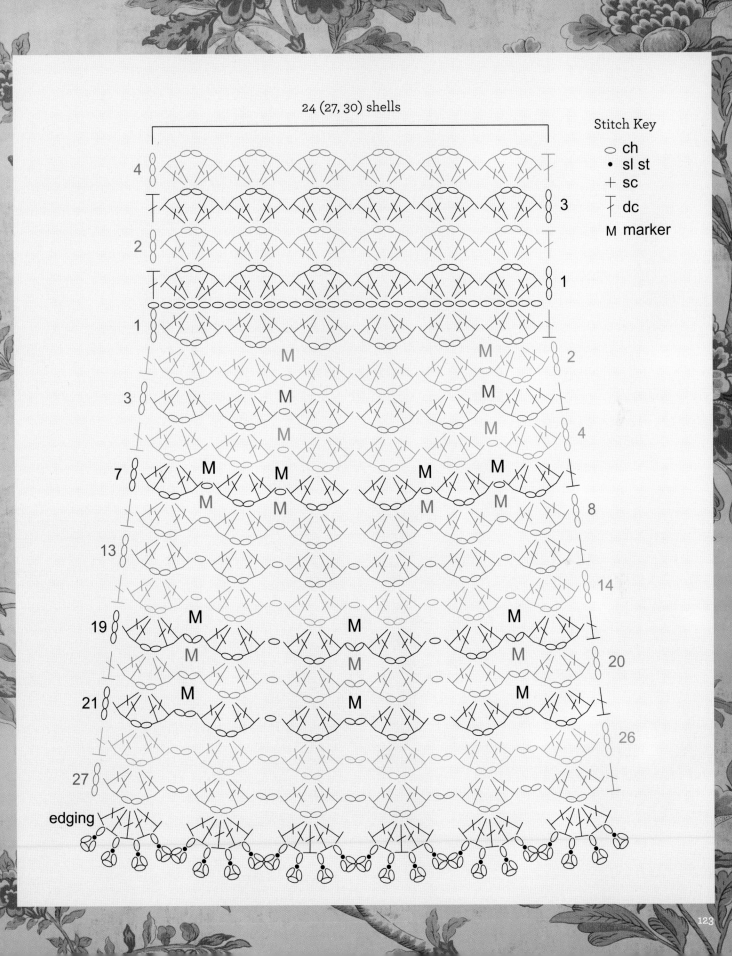

24 (27, 30) shells

Stitch Key

○ ch
• sl st
+ sc
⊤ dc
M marker

Chrysanthemum Shawl

Chrysanthemum Shawl

Circular motifs in shades of burgundy, gold, fuchsia, and yellow create a garden's worth of blooms. Starting each motif at a different point in the color sequence results in a distinct variety of colors.

Designed by Anna Al

Skill Level: ■■□□

Materials

- 6 1¾oz/50g balls (each approx 137yd/125m) of Noro *Silk Garden Lite* (silk/mohair/lambswool) in #2038 burgundy/gold/fuchsia/yellow (3)
- Size G/6 (4mm) crochet hook OR SIZE TO OBTAIN GAUGE
- Yarn needle

Finished Measurements

18" x 65" (45.5cm x 164cm)

Notes

1) Make 108 motifs all from right side without turning.
2) Motifs are connected seamlessly with a slip stitch on rnd 4.
3) Start each new motif by beginning at a new color section of the yarn skein and alternate the skeins for best color distribution.

Gauge

1 motif = 3"/7.5cm diameter using size G/6 (4mm) crochet hook. TAKE TIME TO CHECK GAUGE.

Shawl

First motif

Ch 6; join with sl st in 1st ch to form ring.

Rnd 1 Ch 1, [sc, ch 4] 5 times in ring, sc in ring, ch 1, hdc in 1st sc (counts as ch-sp throughout)—6 ch-sp.

Rnd 2 Ch 1, sc in hdc, [ch 4, sc in next ch-sp] 5 times, ch 1, hdc in 1st sc.

Rnd 3 Ch 1, sc in hdc, [(ch 4, sc) twice in next ch-sp] 5 times; ch 4, sc in next ch-4 sp, ch 1, hdc in 1st sc—12 ch-sp.

Rnd 4 Ch 1, sc in hdc, [ch 4, sc in next ch-sp] 11 times, ch 4, sl st to first sc, fasten off.

Join 2 motifs together

Join 20 A motifs; see layout for location of motifs.

Rnds 1–3 Rep rnds 1–3 of First Motif.

Rnd 4 Ch 1, sc in hdc, ch 2, [sl st in any ch-sp of adjoining motif, ch 2, sc in next ch-sp of this motif] twice, [ch 4, sc in next ch-sp] 9 times, ch 1, hdc in 1st sc, fasten off.

Join 3 motifs together

Join 3 C motifs.

Rnds 1–3 Rep rnds 1–3 of First Motif.

Rnd 4 Ch 1, sc in hdc, *[ch 2, sl st in 2nd ch-sp from join of previous motif one row above, ch 2, sc in next ch-sp of this motif] twice; ch 2, sl st in next ch-sp of previous motif, ch 2, sc in next ch-sp of this motif; rep from * on adjoining motif on current row, [ch 4, sc, in next ch-sp] 7 times, ch 1, hdc in 1st sc, fasten off.

Join 4 motifs together

Join 84 B motifs.

Rnds 1–3 Rep rnds 1–3 of First Motif.

Rnd 4 Ch 1, sc in hdc, *[ch 2, sl st in 2nd ch-sp from join of previous motif one row above, ch 2, sc in next ch-sp of this motif] twice; rep from * on next adjoining motif one row above; rep from * on next adjoining motif on current row, [ch 4, sc, in next ch-sp] 5 times, ch 1, hdc in 1st sc, fasten off.

Assembly

Join motifs one row at a time. In first row, join 14 A motifs and first motif together, creating a row. In second, and subsequent even rows, join one A motif to end of row. Then join 14 B motifs to 2 motifs on row above and previous motif on current row. Join one C motif at opposite end of all even rows. On odd rows, join one A motif to end of row. Then join 14 B motifs to 2 motifs on row above and previous motif on current row. ■

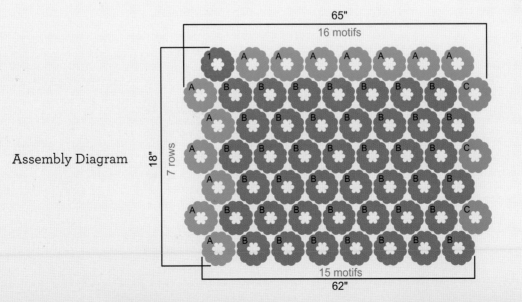

Joining Circle Motifs

Stitch Key

◯ ch
• sl st
+ sc
⊤ hdc

Assembly Diagram

Daisy Chain Scarf

Daisy Chain Scarf

A pretty trefoil stitch forms the body of this playful scarf, which is fringed with daisy motifs.

Designed by Yoko Hatta

Skill Level: ■■□□

Materials

- 3 1¾oz/50g skeins (each approx 198yd/181m) of Noro *Shiraito* (cashmere/angora/wool) in #9 purples/lime/gold/green (**1**)
- Size C/2 (2.75mm) crochet hook OR SIZE TO OBTAIN GAUGE
- Yarn needle

Size

Instructions are written for one size.

Finished Measurements

Length approx 62"/157.5cm long
Width approx 5"/12.5cm wide (not including daisy fringe)
Width approx 7"/18cm wide (including daisy fringe)

Gauge

28 sts and 11 rows to 4"/10cm over pattern st using C/2 (2.75mm) crochet hook. TAKE TIME TO CHECK GAUGE.

Stitch Glossary

Trefoil (Sc, ch 3, sc, ch 5, sc, ch 3, sc) in indicated space.

Scarf

Ch 36.

Row 1 (RS) Sc in 2nd ch from hook, *ch 3, sk next 3 ch, sc in next ch, ch 3, sk next ch, sc in next ch; rep from * across to last 4 ch, ch 3, sk next 3 ch, sc in last ch—11 ch-3 sps.

Row 2 Ch 1, turn, sc in first sc, *ch 3, sk next ch-3 sp, Trefoil in next ch-3 sp; rep from * across to last ch-3 sp, ch 3, sk last ch-3 sp, sc in last sc—5 Trefoils.

Row 3 Ch 7 (counts as tr, ch 3 here and throughout), turn, (sc, ch 3, sc) in ch-5 sp of first Trefoil, *ch 3, (sc, ch 3, sc) in ch-5 sp of next Trefoil; rep from * across to last ch-3 sp, ch 3, sk last ch-3 sp, tr in last sc.

Row 4 Ch 1, turn, sc in first tr, *ch 3, sk next ch-3 sp, Trefoil in next ch-3 sp; rep from * across to turning ch-sp, ch 3, sc in 4th ch of turning ch—5 Trefoils.

Rows 5–168 Rep last 2 rows 82 times.

Row 169 Ch 7, turn, (sc, ch 1, sc) in ch-5 sp of first Trefoil, *ch 3, (sc, ch 1, sc) in ch-5 sp of next Trefoil; rep from * across to ch-3 sp, ch 3, sk last ch-3 sp, tr in last sc. Do not fasten off.

Edging (RS) Ch 1, turn, sc in first st, *ch 3, sk next ch-3 sp, (sc, ch 3, sc) in next ch-1 sp; rep from * across to last ch-3 sp, ch 3, sk last ch-3 sp, (sc, ch 3, sc) in 4th ch of turning ch; rotate piece to work in ends of rows across long side edge, ch 3, sk end of row 169, (sc, ch 3, sc) in end of next row (this should be a row ending with a sc), **ch 3, sk end of next row, (sc, ch 3, sc) in end of next row; rep from ** across to end of row 1, sk end of row 1; working across opposite side of foundation ch, (sc, ch 3, sc) in first ch (at base of first sc of row 1), ch 3, sk next 4 ch, (sc, ch 3, sc) in next ch-1 sp (between sc sts of first row), ***ch 3, sk next 5 ch, (sc, ch 3, sc) in next ch-1 sp; rep from *** across to last 5 ch, ch 3, sc in last ch. Do not fasten off.

Daisy Fringe (RS) Rotate piece to work in ends of rows across rem long side edge, sl st in end of row 1, sl st in end of next row, *ch 16, sl st in 6th ch from hook to form a ring for center of daisy, [ch 2, 3-dc Cl in ring, ch 2, sl st in ring] 5 times (daisy made), ch 10, sk end of next row (this should be a row ending with a tr), sl st in end of next row (this should be a row ending with a sc); rep from * across long edge working last sl st in first sc of edging. Fasten off.

Finishing
Weave in ends. ■

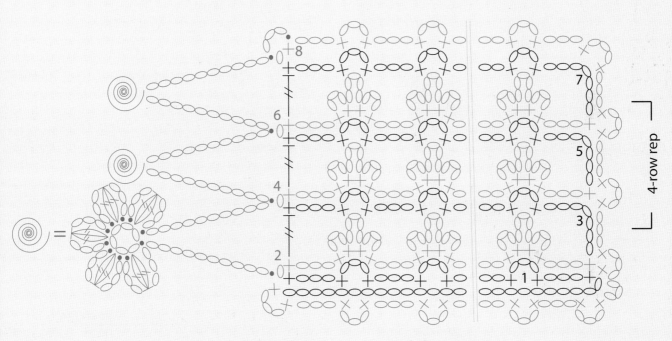

Trefoil Lace Pattern

Stitch Key

- •   sl st
- ○   ch
- +   sc
- 3-dc cl
- tr
- daisy motif

Flower Blossom Purse

Flower Blossom Purse

With its vibrant colors and whimsical motifs, this vintage-style bag conjures up memories of childhood crafts, with a modern twist.

Designed by Yoko Hatta

Skill Level: ■■■□

Materials
- 4 1¾oz/50g skeins (each approx 110yd/100m) of Noro *Kureyon* (wool) in #256 pink/orange/teal (4)
- Size G/6 (4mm) crochet hook OR SIZE TO OBTAIN GAUGE
- Lining fabric (optional)
- Sewing needle and thread (optional)

Size
Instructions are written for one size.

Finished Measurements
Approx 14"/35.5cm wide x 10"/25.5cm deep

Gauge
Motif measures 3¾"/9.5cm square using size G/6 (4mm) crochet hook. TAKE TIME TO CHECK GAUGE.

Stitch Glossary
2-dc Cl (2 double-crochet cluster) Yo, insert hook in indicated st or space and draw up a loop, yo and draw through 2 loops on hook (2 loops remain on hook); yarn over, insert hook in same st or space and draw up a loop, yo and draw through 2 loops on hook, yo and draw through all 3 loops on hook.
pop (4-dc popcorn) 4 dc in indicated stitch, remove loop from hook, insert hook into top of first dc, slip loop back on hook and through first dc (pops st forward).
beg pop (3-dc popcorn) Ch 3, 3 dc in indicated stitch, remove loop from hook, insert hook into top of beg ch, slip loop back on hook and through beg ch (pops st forward).
ch-3 join Ch 1, sl st to adjoining motif's ch-3 sp, ch 1.
ch-5 join Ch 2, sl st to adjoining motif's ch-5 sp, ch 2.

Motif (make 1, join 24)
Ch 4, sl st to first ch to form ring.
Rnd 1 Ch 3 (counts as first dc), work 11 dc in ring, join w sl st to beg ch—12 dc.
Rnd 2 Beg pop in tch, ch 3, *pop in next dc, ch 3; rep from * a total of 10 times, pop in next dc, ch 1, join w hdc to beg pop (hdc, ch 1 counts as ch-3 sp)—12 pop.
Rnd 3 Ch 1, sc in first ch-3 sp (formed by hdc, ch 1 join), ch 3, *(2 dc cl, ch 5, 2 dc cl) in next ch-3 sp (corner), ch 3, sc in next ch-3 sp, ch 5, sc in next ch-3 sp, ch 3; rep from * around, ending sc in last ch-3 sp, ch 5, join to beg sc. Fasten off.

Joining Motifs
Join A motifs
Join 8 A motifs, following assembly diagram.
Rep rnds 1–2 of motif.
Rnd 3 Ch 1, sc in next first ch-3 sp (formed by hdc, ch 1 join), ch 3, (2 dc cluster, ch-5 join, 2 dc cluster) in next ch-3 sp (corner), ch-3 join, sc in next ch-3 sp, ch-5 join, sc in next ch-3 sp, ch-3 join, (2 dc cluster, ch-5 join, 2 dc cluster) in next ch-3 sp, *ch 3, sc in next ch-3

sp, ch 5, sc in next ch-3 sp, ch 3, (2 dc cluster, ch 5, 2 dc cluster) in next ch-3 sp; rep from * around, ending sc in last ch-3 sp, ch 5, join to beg sc. Fasten off.

Join B motifs

Join 16 B motifs, following assembly diagram.

Rep rnds 1–2 of motif.

Rnd 3 Ch 1, sc in next first ch-3 sp (formed by hdc, ch 1 join), ch 3, *(2 dc cluster, ch-5 join, 2 dc cluster) in next ch-3 sp (corner), ch-3 join, sc in next ch-3 sp, ch-5 join, sc in next ch-3 sp, ch-3 join; rep from * once, (2 dc cluster, ch-5 join, 2 dc cluster) in next ch-3 sp, ch 3, sc in next ch-3 sp, ch 5, sc in next ch-3 sp, ch 3, (2 dc cluster, ch 5, 2 dc cluster) in next ch-3 s, ch 3, sc in last ch-3 sp, ch 5, join to beg sc. Fasten off.

Upper Edge Trim

Row 1 With RS facing, join yarn in corner ch-5 sp of motif in top right side w sc. Ch 1, work 25 sc across top edge (with 1 sc in each-sp across, gathers fabric as you crochet).

Row 2 Ch 1, turn, sc in ea sc across.

Rep row 2 for a total of 9 rows. Fasten off.

Rep on opposite side across bottom edge. Fold trim in half with WS facing. Whipstitch last row to first row, fasten off.

Side Trim and Handles

Join yarn to top of upper edge trim at row 4 with sl st, ch 50, sl st to opposite side of trim at other end of row 4.

Repeat on opposite upper edge trim.

Rnd 1 Join yarn to row 4 of upper edge with sl st, *3 sc across row ends of upper trim, 30 sc across side edge (placing 6 sc in each motif, gathers fabric as you crochet), 3 sc across opposite upper trim row ends, sc in each ch across; rep from * once, sl st to first sc—172 sc.

Rnd 2 Ch 1, turn. sc in ea sc around, sl st to first sc.

Rep rnd 2 for 9 rnds total. Fasten off.

Stuff upper trim with leftover yarn. Fold side trim and handles in half with WS facing. Whipstitch last row to first row, stuffing handles with leftover yarn as you sew.

Lining

If desired, cut a piece of lining fabric 15" x 21"/38cm x 28cm. Fold in half widthwise, with RS facing. Sew side seams with ⅜"/1cm seam allowance. Fold down top edge to WS, insert in bag, and sew in place using sewing needle and thread. ∎

Joining Motifs

Stitch Key

ch
sl st
sc
dc
2dc-cl
pop

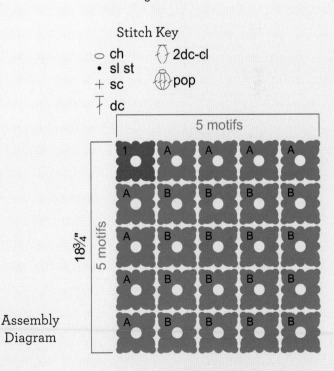

5 motifs

18¾"

5 motifs

Assembly Diagram

Buttons & Flowers Shawl

Buttons & Flowers Shawl

Dozens of flower motifs are joined together to create this lacy shawl. For a longer shawl, simply make and assemble more motifs, arranging them in alternating rows of three and four motifs.

Designed by Linda Voss Plummer

Skill Level: ■■□□

Materials
- 3 3½oz/100g skein (each approx 328yd/300m) of Noro *Silk Garden Sock* (wool/silk/nylon/mohair) in #269 creme/tan/gray ②
- Size F/5 (3.75mm) crochet hook OR SIZE TO OBTAIN GAUGE
- 41 buttons, ⅝" (15mm) diameter
- Yarn needle

Size
Instructions are written for one size.

Finished Measurements
Approx 16"/40.5cm wide (at widest) x 48"/122cm long (at longest)

Note
Shawl is made from 41 six-petal flower motifs. The motifs are arranged as shown in assembly diagram and sewn together. Filler stitching is then worked into the spaces across the long edges, between flower motifs. Then edging is worked around the entire outside edge of the shawl.

Gauge
One flower motif measures about 5"/12.5cm across (at widest), using F/5 (3.75mm) crochet hook. TAKE TIME TO CHECK GAUGE.

Flower Motif (make 41)
Ch 5; join with sl st in first ch to form a ring.
Rnd 1 (RS) Ch 3 (counts as dc here and throughout), dc in ring, ch 1, [2 dc in ring, ch 1] 5 times; join with sl st in top of beg ch—12 dc, and 6 ch-1 sps.
Rnd 2 Sl st in next dc, (sl st, ch 3, dc, ch 3, 2 dc) in first ch-1 sp, (2 dc, ch 3, 2 dc) in each rem ch-1 sp around; join with sl st in top of beg ch—24 dc, and 6 ch-3 sps.
Rnd 3 Sl st in each st to center of first ch-3 sp, ch 10, [sl st in next ch-3 sp, ch 10] 5 times; join with sl st in sl st at base of first ch-10—6 ch-10 sps.
Rnd 4 *10 sc in next ch-10 sp; working over the next sl st, sl st in the ch-3 sp 2 rnds below; rep from * around. Fasten off.

Finishing
The center of each 10-sc group serves as a petal tip. Before assembling shawl, pull gently on the petals to shape each flower motif and ensure that the petal tip is easy to identify. Arrange flower motifs as shown in assembly diagram and sew motifs together at petal tips (center of 10-sc groups).

Long-edge filler stitching
Beg at short end of shawl consisting of 3 motifs (not pointed end), join yarn with sl st in 2nd unjoined petal tip at top of first row of 4 motifs (see assembly diagram), ch 10, sk next petal tip (where two motifs are joined), sl st in next sl st between petals, ch 10, sk next petal tip (where two motifs are joined), sl st in next petal tip (the first unjoined petal tip of next row of 4 motifs), ch 1, turn, 10 sc in first ch-10 sp, sl st in next sl st, 10 sc in next ch-10 sp, ch 1, turn, sl st in first 5 sc of first 10-sc group, sl st in sp between 5th and 6th sc of group, ch 8, sl st in sp at center of next 10-sc group, ch 1, turn, 8 sc in

ch-8 sp, sl st again in sp between 5th and 6th sc of 10-sc group. Fasten off. Rep to fill sps across both long edges.

Outer edging

Rnd 1 (RS) With RS facing, join yarn with sl st in any st, *ch 5, sk next 3 sts, sl st in next st; rep from * around, ch 5; join with sl st in st at base of first ch-5.

Rnd 2 Ch 1, *5 sc in next ch-5 sp, sl st in next sl st; rep from * around. Fasten off.

Blocking

Weave in ends. Wash piece gently, to soften yarn and allow it to "bloom." Spread shawl out on a towel, rug, or blocking mat. Stretch piece gently to open up the lace. Pin points along edge. Allow piece to dry.

Sew one button to center of RS of each motif. ∎

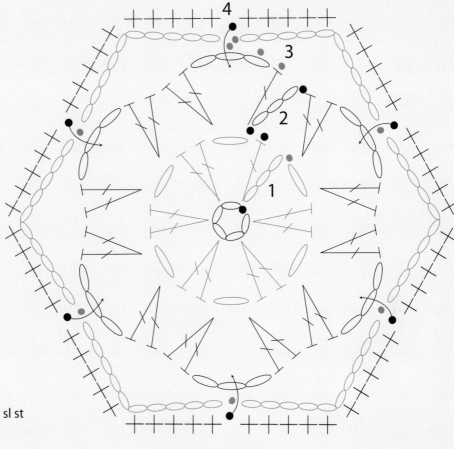

Flower Motif

Stitch Key

- •   sl st
- ↲   sl st worked over sl st and into ch-3 sp
- ⬯   ch
- +   sc
- ⊤   dc

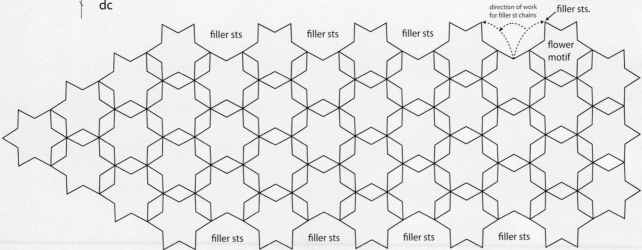

Assembly Diagram

Bias Miniskirt

(Pattern on pages 38–41.)

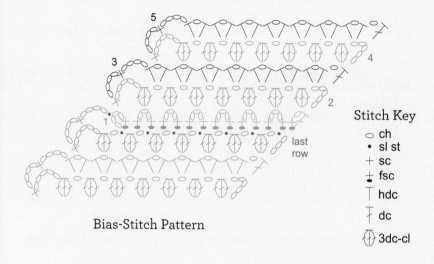

Bias-Stitch Pattern

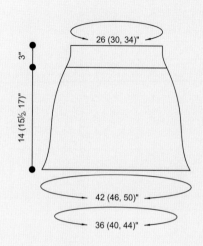

Stitch Key

◯   ch

•   sl st

+   sc

⊥   fsc

⊤   hdc

Ŧ   dc

⬭ 3dc-cl

Short-Row Scarf

(Pattern on pages 74–77.)

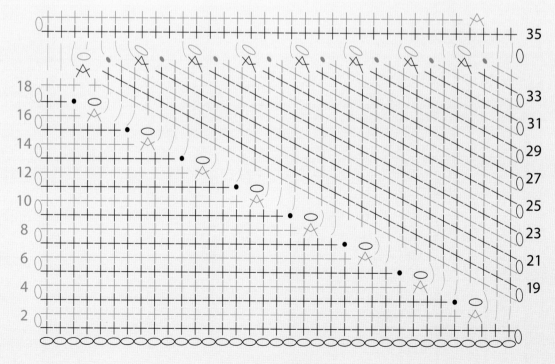

Short-Row Pattern

Shades of Blue Shawl

(Pattern on pages 90–93.)

Joining Motifs Diagram

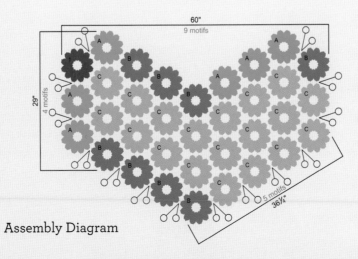

Assembly Diagram

Helpful Information

Abbreviations

approx	approximately
beg	begin; beginning; begins
BPdc	back-post double crochet
ch	chain; chains
cl	cluster
cont	continue; continuing
dc	double crochet
dec	decrease; decreasing
dtr	double treble crochet
foll	follow(s)(ing)
FPdc	front-post double crochet
FPsc	front-post single crochet
grp(s)	group(s)
hdc	half double crochet
inc	increase; increasing
lp(s)	loop(s)
pat(s)	pattern(s)
pm	place maker
pop	popcorn
rem	remain; remains; remaining
rep	repeat
rev sc	reverse single crochet (aka crab stitch)
rnd(s)	round(s)
RS	right side
sc	single crochet
sc2tog	single crochet two together
sk	skip
sl	slip; slipping
sl st	slip stitch
sp	space(s)
st(s)	stitch(es)
tbl	through back loop
t-ch	turning chain
tfl	through front loop
tog	together
tr	treble crochet
trtr	triple treble crochet
WS	wrong side
yo	yarn over hook; make a new stitch by wrapping the yarn around the hook (U.K.: yoh)
[]	rep instructions within brackets as many times as directed
*	rep instructions following an asterisk as many times as indicated

Crochet Hook Sizes

U.S.	Metric	U.S.	Metric
B/1	2.25mm	H/8	5mm
C/2	2.75mm	I/9	5.5mm
D/3	3.25mm	J/10	6mm
E/4	3.5mm	K/10½	6.5mm
F/5	3.75mm	L/11	8mm
G/6	4mm	M/13	9mm
7	4.5mm	N/15	10mm

Skill Levels

■□□□ **Beginner** Ideal first project.

■■□□ **Easy** Basic stitches, minimal shaping, and simple finishing.

■■■□ **Intermediate** For crocheters with some experience. More intricate stitches, shaping, and finishing.

■■■■ **Experienced** For crocheters able to work patterns with complicated shaping and finishing.

Standard Yarn Weight System

Categories of yarn, gauge ranges, and recommended needle and hook sizes

Yarn Weight Symbol & Category Names	0 Lace	1 Super Fine	2 Fine	3 Light	4 Medium	5 Bulky	6 Super Bulky
Type of Yarns in Category	Fingering 10 count crochet thread	Sock, Fingering, Baby	Sport, Baby	DK, Light Worsted	Worsted, Afghan, Aran	Chunky, Craft, Rug	Bulky, Roving
Knit Gauge Range* in Stockinette Stitch to 4 inches	33–40** sts	27–32 sts	23–26 sts	21–24 sts	16–20 sts	12–15 sts	6–11 sts
Recommended Needle in Metric Size Range	1.5–2.25 mm	2.25–3.25 mm	3.25–3.75 mm	3.75–4.5 mm	4.5–5.5 mm	5.5–8 mm	8 mm and larger
Recommended Needle U.S. Size Range	000 to 1	1 to 3	3 to 5	5 to 7	7 to 9	9 to 11	11 and larger
Crochet Gauge* Ranges in Single Crochet to 4 inch	32-42 double crochets**	21–32 sts	16–20 sts	12–17 sts	11–14 sts	8–11 sts	5–9 sts
Recommended Hook in Metric Size Range	Steel*** 1.6–1.4mm Regular hook 2.25 mm	2.25–3.5 mm	3.5–4.5 mm	4.5–5.5 mm	5.5–6.5 mm	6.5–9 mm	9 mm and larger
Recommended Hook U.S. Size Range	Steel*** 6, 7, 8 Regular hook B–1	B–1 to E–4	E–4 to 7	7 to I–9	I–9 to K–10½	K–10½ to M–13	M–13 and larger

* GUIDELINES ONLY: The above reflect the most commonly used gauges and needle or hook sizes for specific yarn categories.

** Lace weight yarns are usually knitted or crocheted on larger needles and hooks to create lacy, openwork patterns. Accordingly, a gauge range is difficult to determine. Always follow the gauge stated in your pattern.

*** Steel crochet hooks are sized differently from regular hooks--the higher the number, the smaller the hook, which is the reverse of regular hook sizing.

This Standards & Guidelines booklet and downloadable symbol artwork are available at: **YarnStandards.com**

Distributors

To locate retailers of Noro yarns, please contact one of the following distributors:

UK & EUROPE
Designer Yarns Ltd.
Units 8–10
Newbridge Industrial Estate
Pitt Street
Keighley BD21 4PQ
UNITED KINGDOM
Tel: +44 (0)1535 664222
Fax: +44 (0)1535 664333
Email: alex@designeryarns.uk.com
www.designeryarns.uk.com

USA
Knitting Fever Inc.
315 Bayview Avenue
Amityville, New York 11701
Tel: 516 546 3600
Fax: 516 546 6871
www.knittingfever.com

CANADA
Diamond Yarn Ltd.
155 Martin Ross Avenue, Unit 3
Toronto, Ontario M3J 2L9
Tel: 001 416 736 6111
Fax: 001 416 736 6112
www.diamondyarn.com

DENMARK
Fancy Knit
Storegade 13
8500 Grenna, Ramten
Tel: +45 59 46 21 89
Fax: +45 59 46 80 18
Email: kelly@fancyknitdanmark.com

ICELAND
Stokurinn
Laugavegi 59
101 Reykjavik
Tel: 354 551 8258
Fax: 354 562 8252
Email: storkurinn@storkurinn.is

**GERMANY/AUSTRIA/
SWITZERLAND/BELGIUM/
NETHERLANDS/LUXEMBOURG**
Designer Yarns (Deutschland) GMBH
Welserstrasse 10g, D-51149 Koln
GERMANY
Tel: +49 (0) 2203 1021910
Fax: +49 (0) 2203 1023551
Email: info@designeryarns.de

SWEDEN
Hamilton Yarns
Storgatan 14, 64730 Mariefred
Tel/Fax: +46 (0) 1591 2006
www.hamiltondesign.biz

FINLAND
Eiran Tukku
Makelankatu 54B, 00510 Helsinki
Tel: +358 503460575
Email: maria.hellbom@eirantukku.fi

NORWAY
Viking of Norway
Bygdaveien 63
4333 Oltedal
Tel: +47 51611660
Fax: +47 51616235
Email: post@viking-garn.no
www.viking-garn.no

POLAND
Mari Yarn Mariola Rychel
Ul. Akacjowa 8, Smolec
55-080 Katy Wroclawskie
Tel: +48 668 29 30 35
Email: sklep@e-dziewiarka.pl

KOREA
Ann Knitting
1402 Dongjin Building
735-6 Gyomun-dong
Guri-si Gyeonggi-do 471-020
Tel: +82 70 4367 2767
Fax: 82 2 6937 0577
Email: tedd@annknitting.com

FRANCE
Plassard Diffusion
La Filature
71800 Varennes-sous-Dun
Tel: +33 (0) 385282828
Fax: +33 (0) 385282829
Email: info@laines-plassard.com

AUSTRALIA/NEW ZEALAND
Prestige Yarns Pty Ltd.
P.O. Box 39
Bulli, New South Wales 2516
AUSTRALIA
Tel: +61 24 285 6669
Email: info@prestigeyarns.com
www.prestigeyarns.com

SPAIN
Castelltort
Botanica 137–139
Polig. Ind. Pedrosa
08908 L'Hospitalet
Tel: +93 268 36 11
Fax: +34 (0) 93 218 6694
Email: mjose@castelltort.com

JAPAN
Eisaku Noro & Co Ltd.
55 Shimoda Ohibino Azaichou
Ichinomiya, Aichi 491 0105
Tel: +81 586 51 3113
Fax: +81 586 51 2625
Email: noro@io.ocn.ne.jp
www.eisakunoro.com

RUSSIA
Fashion Needlework
Evgenia Rodina, Ul. Nalichnaya, 27
St. Petersburg 199226
Tel: +7 (812) 928-17-39,
(812) 350-56-76, (911) 988-60-03
Email: knitting.info@gmail.com
www.fashion-rukodelie.ru